SLAYING ORLANDO

Curated by Leigh M. Clark

Aurora Corialis Publishing

Pittsburgh, PA

Printed in the United States of America
Edited by: Renee Picard, Aurora Corialis Publishing
Cover Design: Leigh M. Clark
Paperback ISBN: 978-1-958481-66-0
Ebook ISBN: 978-1-958481-67-7

Table of Contents

Introduction i

    Leigh M. Clark i

From Corporate Dreams to Entrepreneurial Fire: A Journey of
Reinvention 1

    Irina Zakharchenko 1

The Modern Alchemy of Power, Peace, and Profit 11

    Florencia "Flo 2.0" Tarque 11

Turning Pain into Purpose: The Story of Celena Adams 21

    Celena Adams 21

Slaying Orlando 27

    Alyce Bartolomeo 27

One Step Further 31

    Katie Bean 31

Rewriting My Story: From Brokenness to Building Hope 39

    Ashley Bedford 39

The Strength of Scars: from Chaos to Purpose 45

    Katherine Carpio 45

Two Oaths, One Purpose: How I Became a Healer, a Citizen, and
the Architect of a Life I Once Only Imagined 53

    Dr. Elizabeta Cokovska 53

Who Cares What They Said 61

    Shay Edwards 61

My Story 69

    Cathy McCaw Engelman 69

Brushstrokes of Independence: An Artist's Journey 75

Sally Evans 75

A Life Designed with Grace 83

DeDe DeWine Holloway 83

The Basement of the Kremlin...91

Rinat Halon Neal 91

Legacy of Grace, Threads of Strength 99

Endsley Hewitt.. 99

The Escape Artist...107

Ansley Highland..107

From Wounds to Breath, From Silence to Light..................... 115

Lizbeth Jimenez... 115

Becoming HER: The Seed That Needed the Right Environment
....123

Leandrea Long 123

Strength in the Struggle: Building Body Construct and Building
Myself.. 131

Lori-Ann Marchese 131

The Light Side of Leadership 139

Lady Alisha Martin 139

Beyond the Runway: When Style, Story, and Compassion Walk
Hand in Hand 145

Josie NeJame 145

From Smiles to Styles: Mom, Wife, Entrepreneur—One Manicure
at a Time 151

Kasia Pukeca 151

Steering from Heaven: A Daughter's Journey of Love, Loss, and
Purpose 159

Christina Pinto Rogers, CFP® 159

The Fine Art of Estate Sales and Second Chances 167

Melissa Sullivan 167

A Journey Built on Love, Service, and Transformation 175

Shiela Wyatt 175

Beauty From Ashes 183

Bree Holbrook 183

About the Curator, Leigh M. Clark 189

Introduction

Leigh M. Clark

The first time I went to Orlando, I was ten years old.

It was with my nana—one of the kindest people you'll ever meet—and my uncle Jack, who was, without question, one of the wildest.

It was my first time ever setting foot in Florida. The drive felt endless, but I didn't care. I pressed my face against the window and stared out at the palm trees swaying along the highway. I'd never seen anything like them. They didn't just stand there—they danced. They looked like exclamation points in the sky, stretching toward the sun.

That trip was everything a ten-year-old could want. Disney, Universal, roller coasters, laughter that carried through the night. But even then, what I remember most wasn't the rides. It was the feeling. The warmth. The sunlight bouncing off water. The way strangers smiled at you. Orlando felt alive, like it was humming with something bigger—like possibility itself lived there.

And then there was the moment Jack took us into a Publix. Nana, soft-spoken and endlessly kind, was in her element, chatting with people as if she'd known them forever. My uncle was already cracking jokes with the bakery clerk. I was just... taking it all in. The bright aisles, the smell of fresh bread, the calm buzz of people moving with purpose. Something about it felt safe. Familiar. Like a memory I didn't know I was making.

At ten years old, I fell in love with Florida without even realizing it.

Losing the Spark, Finding It Again

Fast-forward a couple of decades — New York City.

I loved that city. Still do. But when the 2008 recession hit, it hit hard. It stripped everything down—the energy, the optimism, the sense of security. I was in my twenties, burning the candle at both ends, and then the candle holder melted too.

So, in 2010, I left. Not because I had some perfect plan, but because I needed air. I needed quiet. I needed to find whatever piece of peace I'd lost somewhere between conference calls and subway delays.

And when I thought about where peace had last found me, I remembered those palm trees.

Florida.

I came here chasing that same stillness I'd felt as a child—the sunlight filtering through the palms, the sense that the world slowed down just long enough for you to breathe again.

The Orlando Chapter

By 2012, I was working for a company called LivingSocial — which would later become Groupon. I was the sales manager for Orlando, leading a team of eight of the most talented, driven people I've ever worked with.

We didn't have an office. Remote work wasn't even a buzzword yet, but we were already living it. My team worked across Central Florida — Lake Mary to Kissimmee, Lake Nona to Clermont. And a few days a week, I'd make the three-hour drive up from the Gulf Coast to see them.

I'd leave around seven a.m., roll into Orlando by ten, meet with clients, grab lunch with my team, and then head home in time for dinner. It was a grind, sure, but it didn't feel like one. The drive itself became its own kind of meditation — watching the landscape change, the palms coming back into view, reminding me that I was exactly where I was supposed to be.

Our meetings were never formal. We'd grab sushi in Winter Park, brainstorm at coffee shops in College Park, or meet at Universal — sometimes even Disney. We'd talk about strategy over soy sauce, goals between roller-coaster laughter, new partnerships while watching fireworks. We worked hard, but we also lived.

Those were some of my favorite years. I learned that business could be built on connection, not competition.

The Orlando Most People Don't See

When you're in a city long enough, you start to know it by its textures.

Lake Mary — polished and practical.

Lake Nona — modern, futuristic, full of innovation.

Kissimmee — heart and hustle.

Clermont — rolling hills that feel like a secret Florida doesn't want you to find.

Lakeland — a coin toss between Tampa and Orlando depending on the day.

But under all of that, there's a pulse that never makes the travel brochures. It's the Orlando that exists between the parks—the one built by people who stay when the tourists leave.

The women here, especially, impressed me. Artists' passions turning into global brands. Fashion designers using their talent to fund cancer research. Former TV personalities pivoting into purpose-driven ventures. Women who'd faced loss, burnout, reinvention—and came out the other side more certain of themselves.

That's the Orlando I fell in love with all over again. Not the glitter, but the grit.

Behind the Magic

When we'd meet inside Universal or Disney, I used to love catching a glimpse of the backstage areas—the places the tourists never see. There's a strange beauty in the contrast between the fantasy and the machinery that makes it work. It reminded me a lot of life—especially women's lives. We make the magic look effortless, but behind it is structure, discipline, and sleepless nights.

Orlando taught me that the magic isn't fake. It's just built. Carefully, intentionally, by people who believe in joy enough to manufacture it.

And maybe that's why this city resonated so deeply with me. It's both wonder and work. It's fantasy and foundation.

Reclaiming Peace

When I started the Slay the USA series in 2023, I wanted to capture the soul of each city through the women who define it—the thinkers, dreamers, leaders, doers. Orlando became our tenth book, and in so many ways, it feels like the perfect symbol of what this movement is about: resilience, rebirth, and quiet power.

Because Orlando isn't just a city of lights and laughter. It's a place that lets you evolve. You can arrive burned out, heart-tired, unsure of your next move—and somehow, the palms still sway for you. The sunsets still wait for you. The warmth still welcomes you home.

Full Circle, Again

Sometimes I think back to that ten-year-old girl in the backseat, staring out the window, wide-eyed at the palm trees. She didn't know she'd come back here decades later, searching for that same calm. But she did.

And when I stand in Orlando now—at an author brunch, or an art show, or just walking through Lake Eola with a cup of coffee—I still feel it. That same wonder. That same reminder that life can surprise you. That peace doesn't have to mean stillness. It can mean motion, too—when you're moving toward something that finally feels right.

So, welcome to Orlando.

Welcome to the City Beautiful, the city that breaks you open just enough to let the light in.

And to the women who make it shine: this one's for you.

From Corporate Dreams to Entrepreneurial Fire: A Journey of Reinvention

Irina Zakharchenko

I was standing in the middle of Madison Avenue, sirens wailing and horns blaring around me, clutching a pair of emergency shoes from a boutique I'd just ducked into. My broken heel had given way under the relentless pace of another frantic day. My BlackBerry was buzzing incessantly, another crisis, another meeting I had to make before my CEO arrived. The chaos of Manhattan swirled around me, construction noise, taxi horns, the thunderous rumble of the subway beneath my feet as I ran toward the station, my heart pounding not from the sprint but from a realization that would take me years to fully understand: I was living someone else's definition of success.

That moment in 2007, racing through the concrete jungle in a designer suit with a shattered shoe, would become the first crack in the perfect corporate picture I'd built around myself. But I didn't know it then. I was too busy surviving, too busy proving that a woman from Eastern Europe with an Australian accent could belong in the boardrooms of Fortune 10 companies.

The Foundation of Dreams

My journey began long before that busy day in Manhattan. It started in Ukraine, where I learned my first lesson about resilience from watching my mother navigate a world that wasn't always kind. When we moved to Australia, I discovered that reinvention wasn't just possible, it was necessary. Each country taught me a different language of survival, a different way of seeing opportunity in uncertainty.

In Australia, I found my voice working as an executive assistant to CEOs of major companies. I wasn't just answering phones or scheduling meetings; I was building systems, analyzing data, and quietly proving that the woman behind the scenes could see patterns others missed. When I automated an entire supply chain using nothing but spreadsheets and Microsoft Access years before anyone was talking about AI, I felt the first spark of what would become my entrepreneurial fire.

But America called to me with promises I couldn't resist. In 2004, my husband and I arrived in Staten Island with two suitcases and dreams bigger than our bank account to move into a studio apartment. I remember walking into that first coffee shop in Staten Island, speaking what I thought was perfect English, only to be met with confused stares. My Australian accent, my confidence, even my experience—none of it translated the way I expected.

"You don't have American experience," became the refrain that haunted my early job searches. But life has a way of placing angels in unexpected places. A medical healthcare agency in Brooklyn became my classroom, where I learned not just American business practices, but the art of starting over without losing yourself in the process.

The Corporate Climb

The call came on a Tuesday in 2007. "We need someone like you," the recruiter said. "International background, bilingual, legal and business experience." By Thursday, I was sitting across from executives at a global conglomerate with $26.8 billion in revenue, trying not to let my hands shake as they offered me a role supporting a Forbes-ranked CEO.

Those years in Manhattan were intoxicating and exhausting in equal measure. I managed multi-million-dollar budgets, managed government international affairs, experienced travel that spanned continents, and sat in meetings where decisions worth millions were made over lunch. I learned to speak the language of someone who was power-confident, precise, and always three steps ahead.

But power came with a price I wasn't prepared to pay. The two-hour commute each way. The BlackBerry that never slept. The winter months when I left home in darkness and returned after sunset, feeling like I was missing my own life. My son was born in 2008, and suddenly the stakes weren't just about my career; they were about the kind of mother I wanted to be.

When Johnson & Johnson offered me a chance to pivot into HR in 2015, I felt the universe opening a door. Here was a company whose credo aligned with my values, where I could blend my love of data with my passion for people. For six years, I thrived in that environment, building programs that touched thousands of employees globally, working on initiatives that mattered.

I thought I had found my forever home.

The Shattering

August 2021. The words "position eliminated" echoed through the video call like a death sentence. In the span of thirty minutes, the corporate identity I'd spent years building crumbled beneath my feet. My husband's job was also on shaky ground. We'd just bought a house in Orlando. My son was starting middle school.

I sat in my home office, the same space where I'd successfully led remote teams through the early days of COVID, and felt like I was suffocating. Everything I'd built my life around was gone. My network, my future plans, my sense of self, all of it had been tied to a job that no longer existed.

That night, I locked myself in the bathroom and cried until I had no tears left. Then I looked at myself in the mirror and saw something I hadn't expected: not defeat, but defiance. Not the end, but a beginning.

"Build your life around your life, not your job," became my mantra as I picked up the pieces.

The Leap of Faith

The job offer from a respectable biotech company in California should have been an easy yes. It was appealing, it was familiar, it was everything I knew how to do well. But when my thirteen-year-old son looked at me over dinner and said, "Mom, when you can be better in a smaller company instead of average in a huge company, I think you should take the opportunity to be better, even if it's risky. Daddy and I will support you." I knew the universe was speaking through him.

The startup world was revelation and reckoning all at once. No safety nets, no corporate policies to hide behind, just pure hustle and the intoxicating possibility of building something from a clean slate. I learned to move at the speed of innovation, to make decisions with incomplete information, to fail fast and pivot faster.

But perhaps more importantly, I learned that my corporate experience wasn't something to shed; it was my secret weapon. While other startup employees were figuring out how to scale, I already knew how to build systems that could handle growth. While they were learning about compliance and governance, I was implementing frameworks that would protect the company as it expanded.

When the company faced financial challenges in early 2024, I wasn't devastated like I'd been after Johnson & Johnson. I was energized. Because now I knew something I'd never known before: I wasn't meant to be an employee. I was meant to be a builder.

The Birth of ApolloRise

My husband had been talking about AI and automation long before ChatGPT made headlines, back when people thought he was crazy for believing machines could transform business. "You have all the knowledge, resilience, passion, and drive to make this work," he told me over coffee one morning. "Here's the idea. Now go execute it."

And that's how DocsDNA was born, a company that would eventually merge into ApolloRise. Standing in our kitchen that day, I felt the same electricity I'd experienced in that Brooklyn healthcare agency years earlier when I built my first automated system. The same spark that had carried me through Manhattan boardrooms and New Jersey corporate offices.

But this time, it was different. This time, I wasn't building someone else's vision. I was creating my own.

The early days were terrifying and thrilling. Building proprietary AI software worth millions. Securing more than one thousand B2C clients and dozens of B2B relationships across the United States and Latin America within our first year. Growing a team of more than fifty professionals who believed in our mission as passionately as I did.

Every late-night reiteration and coding session, every investor pitch, every moment of doubt was balanced by the intoxicating realization that I was exactly where I was meant to be. Not just surviving in someone else's company, but thriving in my own.

Finding My Tribe

The breakthrough came when I joined Women in Tech & Entrepreneurs in Orlando in early 2025. Suddenly, I wasn't just building a company, I was part of a movement. As senior chapter chair, I found myself mentoring other women who were standing where I had stood just years earlier: at the crossroads between safety and possibility, between someone else's vision and their own.

Orlando's tech ecosystem embraced me in ways I'd never experienced in corporate America. Here, my accent wasn't something to overcome; it was part of my story. My winding path wasn't a liability; it was proof that success comes in many forms. My age wasn't a limitation; it was wisdom earned through fire.

When Forbes Business Council invited me to join as a thought leader, when Marquis Who's Who honored me as a 2025 listee, I realized something profound: I wasn't just building a company anymore. I was building a legacy.

The View from Here

Today, as co-founder and COO of ApolloRise, I wake up every morning knowing that everything I've experienced, every broken heel, every eliminated position, every moment of doubt, was preparing me for this. We're transforming procurement and sourcing through AI-driven intelligence, but we're really doing something deeper: we're proving that human expertise amplified by technology can create possibilities we never imagined.

When I speak to young women just starting their careers, or to women my age contemplating their second act, I see myself in their eyes, that mixture of hunger and uncertainty, ambition and fear. I tell them about the busy day in Manhattan, about the studio apartment in Staten Island, about the corporate dreams that died so entrepreneurial fire could be born.

But mostly, I tell them this: your path doesn't have to look like anyone else's. The detours aren't delays; they're preparation. The setbacks aren't endings; they're setups for comebacks you can't even imagine yet.

I think about my younger self, clutching those emergency shoes on Madison Avenue, worried about being late to someone else's meeting. If I could go back and whisper in her ear, I'd tell her to slow down, to pay attention, to trust that every step—even the broken ones—was leading somewhere beautiful.

I'd tell her that the woman she's becoming is worth every struggle she's about to face.

And to you, reading this story, wondering if it's too late to start over, if you're too old to dream new dreams, if your accent is too thick or your path too unconventional, I want you to know something: If I can do it, you can too. Anything is possible when you set yourself up for success by believing in the power of your own reinvention.

Your broken heel moment is coming. When it does, don't just survive it.

Use it to run toward the life you're meant to live.

About Irina

Irina Zakharchenko is a transformational leader whose journey spans continents, industries, and a lifetime of reinvention. Born in Ukraine and raised between there and Australia, she learned early that resilience and curiosity could open doors to new worlds. Those lessons carried her to New York City, where she worked alongside Fortune 10 executives, and then to New Jersey, where she spent over two decades helping organizations grow and transform in healthcare, biotech, and technology.

Her path has never been a straight line, but that is where her strength lies. Irina has built her career by embracing change, stepping boldly into uncertainty, and turning challenges into opportunities. When life brought her to Central Florida, she reinvented herself once again, this time as an entrepreneur. Today, as the co-founder and COO of ApolloRise, she leads with vision and heart, helping businesses unlock new possibilities by blending people, data, and innovation.

Beyond her role as an executive, Irina is deeply committed to lifting others. She serves as senior chapter chair for Women in Tech & Entrepreneurs in Orlando, mentoring and empowering women to step into leadership and build the future on their own terms. She is also a proud member of the Forbes Business Council, where she shares her global insights on AI adoption, leadership, resilience, and the future of work.

Irina's story is proof that reinvention is possible at every stage of life. She is not only building companies, she is building pathways for others to rise, showing women everywhere that if she can do it, so can you.

LinkedIn - https://www.linkedin.com/in/irinazprocuretech/
Forbes Business Council -
https://councils.forbes.com/profile/Irina-Zakharchenko-Co-Founder-COO-ApolloRise-Tech/73fbbd34-d997-45cc-a755-4baa96ea2af9
Instagram - @btb_beyondthebadge
https://apollorise.tech

The Modern Alchemy of Power, Peace, and Profit

Florencia "Flo 2.0" Tarque

Let's get something straight. I didn't come back to write another emotional redemption story.

I've almost died three times in the past two years and I'm convinced there's a reason the Lord hasn't taken me out yet. Apparently, He's still got me on payroll, but He's the best, so I don't mind working overtime.

Slaying isn't about hustle anymore. It's about systems, energy, precision, and faith—the kind that reminds you that purpose has a pulse, and as long as yours is still beating, you've got work to do.

The New Definition of "Slay"

Once upon a time, slaying meant grinding until your eyelash extensions fell off. Now it's about "flo" (pun intended) and intelligent execution.

You don't need to be everywhere and control everything; you need to build things that move without you and, most importantly, while you rest.

Slaying today means designing systems that outwork you, content that outlives you, and offers that outsell you. It's not just girl-bossing anymore. It's architecting.

How I Built a Machine That Prints Momentum

In six months, I closed over eight figures in business, not because I'm the loudest in the room, but because I'm the most strategic.

Heavys Development: a roofing company I scaled through AI, branding, Ask Engine Optimization, and automation systems that cut costs, tripled speed, and built trust directly with the labor source.

Dr. Fix It: my family's handyman company, launched in Orlando with a one-hundred-property portfolio in thirty days, offering stress-free short-term-rental maintenance for property management companies.

CarbonAi: my personal AI agency, generating over one hundred thousand dollars' profit in three months while helping businesses across America enter the new digital era through Ask Engine Optimization, AI-powered websites, branding, lead generation, and recruiting. In 2025 alone, our clients produced over forty million dollars in home-services, insurance, call centers, real estate, etc.

That didn't happen because of luck. It happened because I stopped doing everything manually. I stopped acting like a soldier and started thinking like a general.

After years in AI, since 2019, I've refined the blueprint and now dominate the artificial intelligence space with new, more powerful tools—one that's literally printing results for me and my clients. It's not hype; it's a formula that converts intelligence into income.

Free Gold #1: AI Isn't Just a Tool — It's Leverage

People ask, "How do you actually make money with AI?"

Here's the real question: *What parts of your business steal your time but don't grow your revenue?*

That's where your gold is.

Start with the bottlenecks, the repetitive, time-sucking tasks that drain your creativity. Emails, proposals, quotes, follow-ups, scheduling, customer updates, all of it can be automated in under a week with the right workflow.

AI doesn't replace people; it empowers them. It removes friction so humans can do what humans do best: create, connect, and close.

That's how I turned a roofing company into a data-driven sales engine, a handyman service into a turnkey property brand, and consulting into passive income. You don't need more staff, you need a smarter process.

Free Gold #2: The Law of Intelligent Abundance

Abundance isn't about having more; it's about multiplying what already works.

AI amplifies who you are. If you're organized, it makes you unstoppable. If you're chaotic, it multiplies the mess. Trust me, I would know. My ADHD is on full throttle, especially after quitting Adderall three years ago.

Before you automate, decide what you want your systems to create, more time, more profit, or more peace. Build your machine around the goal, not your ego.

Free Gold #3: How to Make Your Business Sell Without Selling

Sales today is psychology, not pressure.

Every AI system I build runs on one principle: understand people, then let technology scale the connection.

Provide immediate value. People buy trust before they buy services.

Create connection. Use automation to communicate personally, not generically.

Convert without chasing. Let your systems follow up while you focus on strategy.

Close and nurture. Make clients feel taken care of before they even pay you.

That's how I built companies that never stop growing through referrals, because people remember how the experience *felt*.

And we always have a "who." Business is built on relationships; connections are the real currency.

Free Gold #4: Energy Is the New KPI

Your true performance metric isn't revenue. It's your energy, generated and amplified by what status your nervous system is in.

You can't scale from survival mode.

The most successful entrepreneurs aren't the busiest; they're the calmest. I protect my energy like equity because it is.

Every meeting, deal, or partnership gets filtered through one question: *Does this expand me or drain me?* If it drains me, it doesn't deserve me.

When you protect your peace like profit, you start attracting both, even when you're not trying.

Free Gold #5: Systems Create Freedom, Not Shackles

Freedom isn't time off; it's control over your time.

I travel, work part-time, and run multiple companies, not because I'm balanced, but because I built leverage. I don't just automate tasks; I automate decisions.

Systems don't make you less human. They make you less busy being a stressed human. That's where real freedom begins.

The Modern Feminine Edge

For years, I led from my masculine: logic, control, execution. It worked, until it didn't.

When I started blending it with the feminine—intuition, magnetism, and flow—I stopped chasing opportunity and started attracting it.

The most powerful women I know don't scream power. They radiate it. They walk into rooms knowing everything they've built will still be running when they leave, because their systems are doing the talking.

Structure + Surrender = Power that Scales.

Free Gold #6: Build Once, Sell Forever

AI is the first revolution that lets you clone yourself without losing your sanity.

If you teach something, record it.

If you repeat something, automate it.

If you prove something, package it.

Stop trading time for transformation. Build assets that outlive you.

I don't build businesses anymore; I build blueprints.

Your goal isn't to be the hardest worker in the room, it's to build a room that works harder without you in it.

Free Gold #7: The Next Digital Gold Rush — AEO, AI Communication, & Agency Creation

SEO is old money. AEO is new wealth.

While most companies still fight for Google rankings, I'm building brands that rank inside ChatGPT, Bard, Gemini, Alexa, and every AI-driven search engine defining the next decade.

Answer Engine Optimization (AEO) is the biggest digital opportunity since SEO's birth. When SEO exploded, early adopters became millionaires. Now AI search is replacing browsers. By 2026, over half of all searches will happen through conversational AI, not search bars.

If your business isn't structured for AI to understand and recommend it, it's already behind.

Through **CarbonAi**, I'm leading this new wave, launching AEO-optimized businesses from the USA to the UK, Dubai to Colombia, making brands answerable, not just searchable.

My clients dominate AI visibility because I engineer frameworks that feed data directly into large language models, metadata, conversational schema, and FAQ content that makes AI choose them first.

It's like buying beachfront property before everyone realizes the ocean's moving.

And I'm not just doing this for corporations. I'm building **AI agencies for individuals**, consultants, marketers, sales professionals, giving them my exact blueprint, training them, building their systems, and guaranteeing their first clients so they see an immediate ROI.

Within thirty days, they're running profitable agencies delivering the same AI recruiting systems, CRM automations, AI callers for specific niches, and AEO frameworks that have generated seven-figure consulting deals.

This wave isn't about who works hardest, it's about who sees where attention is going and builds the road before everyone else drives on it.

If SEO was the gold rush, AEO is the blockchain, and AI communication is the new Wall Street. My clients are building the foundations everyone else will rent from later.

Free Gold #8: The Power Behind the Builder

No empire is built in isolation; every visionary needs a foundation of strength around them.

First and always, God. Every empire I build, every deal I close, rests on the foundation of faith. If I were to thank just one source of strength, it begins with Him. Because when the stakes got real, I realized purpose is more powerful than profit.

Then there's my family, Alejandro, Natalia, and Kiki. They're the hardest-working people I know, the reason I could expand into a one hundred-property portfolio in our first month, the heartbeat behind every win. Their discipline, their sweat, their loyalty built the bedrock of what I get to do today. Success without gratitude is just noise.

Next, I honor Alberto Nikodimov, my partner and the owner of Memories Vacation Home Management. He leads with calm, clarity, and a kind of quiet power that creates space for me to grow and shine. When a man stands confidently in purpose and peace, the woman beside him doesn't just follow, she multiplies.

And finally, I pay tribute to a personal hero of mine, whom out of respect I will keep anonymous. His life was marked by voice, conviction, and relentless pursuit of purpose. His passing illuminated something in me: the call to live more boldly, lead with more integrity, and never shrink because comfort is tempting and legacy is not guaranteed. He reminded me that conviction outlives comfort and that when we stop having hard conversations and disagreements, we lose.

No empire stands alone. I may be the architect, but these pillars are my blueprint: God first, family always, support that elevates, and inspiration that challenges. I'll never forget the hands that helped me build.

The Final Flex

Slaying isn't about killing it anymore; it's about creating it—opportunity, alignment, and freedom. Creating calm in chaos. Creating proof that women can scale empires and still have peace, love, and a perfect manicure.

Here's your takeaway, **your final gold**:

You don't need more hours; you need better systems. You don't need more followers; you need stronger alignment. You don't need to prove you can do it alone; you need to prove you can build something that doesn't depend on you.

That's the real flex. Because the next generation of slayers won't be the loudest, they'll be the ones whose lives run like software: powerful, effortless, and beautifully designed.

And if thirty-year-old me could give twenty-year-old me a tip? *Listen to your intuition sooner. Walk into rooms that challenge you instead of clubs that drain you. Network like your future depends on it, and maybe buy more XRP a little earlier.*

About Florencia

Florencia Tarque doesn't just write about success, she reverse-engineers it. In *Slaying Sarasota*, she taught readers how to build empires out of chaos. In *Slaying Orlando*, she proves what happens when intelligence meets alignment.

A world traveler and self-proclaimed system architect to the ambitious, Florencia has spent years building the machines behind the momentum, turning cluttered ideas into million-dollar systems and everyday people into powerful brands. Known globally as one of the best connectors in business, she's the person you call when you need the who, the what, and the how to make something happen fast.

Her chapter isn't a pep talk, it's a blueprint. It's for women who are done glorifying exhaustion and ready to replace hustle with harmony, chaos with clarity, and effort with intelligence. With the humor of someone who's nearly died three times and still closed seven-figure deals in heels, Florencia teaches that faith, flow, and precision can coexist, and when they do, they create freedom that no paycheck can buy.

At her core, she's not just building systems; she's building believers. Because the new definition of "slaying" isn't about conquering the world, it's about designing one that works beautifully, faithfully, and powerfully for you.

Turning Pain into Purpose: The Story of Celena Adams

Celena Adams

I didn't have time to process what was happening.

Just days after turning twenty-nine, only three weeks into newlywed life, I woke up with the left side of my body numb, my words slurring, and my vision blurring like I was going cross-eyed. What should have been one of the happiest seasons of my life quickly turned into a living nightmare.

Paramedics rushed me to the hospital after I collapsed, and it was in the ambulance that I first heard the words: *"There's a mass on your brain."* It had completely overtaken the entire left side.

They found two brain tumors, one that immediately had to be removed.

The nurses thought I had hit my head. My sister-in-law, a nurse practitioner, told my husband Justin over the phone that I had a fifty/fifty chance of living, that I was going downhill fast. My words were coming out wrong, mixing Cs with 6s. And I was slipping quickly.

I was uninsured, recently unemployed, and terrified. On the same day I was rushed into emergency brain surgery, I lost my executive-level job. They never even paid me my last check. At the time, insurance was something we simply couldn't afford.

And yet, God made a way.

Worshipping in the Valley

In those darkest moments, I worshiped. I turned on praise music, sang through the pain, and wept in His presence. Worship was how I made it through the nights. I would hold Justin's hand and whisper prayers when I couldn't get out of bed.

My favorite verse became my daily anthem:

"Trust in the Lord with all your heart, and lean not on your own understanding. In all your ways acknowledge Him, and He shall direct your paths." – Proverbs 3:5-6

I couldn't understand any of it. But I chose to trust Him anyway. And He kept showing up.

I remember telling my husband, *"If I don't make it, maybe this is how God wants to use me, to bring others to Him. And if I do survive, then that's proof of His healing. Either way, my purpose isn't over."*

Healing Isn't Always Pretty

Brain surgery was only the beginning. After the operation, I had to learn how to walk again. I lost ten pounds due to a jaw muscle incision that made eating difficult. I couldn't shower or use the bathroom on my own. I couldn't even look in the mirror for a week after shaving off what was left of my hair.

And yet, shaving my head felt oddly liberating. As I stared at the woman staring back at me, I no longer saw a victim; I saw a fighter.

Justin was my anchor. He never left my side. He helped me walk, shower, eat, stretch, and build up my strength again. He made sure I had nutritious meals, kept track of my supplements, and believed in my healing even when I didn't. He called me beautiful even when I felt broken. His love reminded me of Christ's love: sacrificial, steady, and sure.

Still, healing was not linear. There were nights I didn't want to go on. I experienced depression so deep, I wondered if I would ever see the light again. I had moments of suicidal thoughts. That pain, that silence, it was a place I wouldn't wish on anyone.

Doctors wanted to put me through radiation, but it would've increased the risk of another tumor. I chose to pursue a more natural route, and I don't regret it.

A New Kind of Calling

During my bed rest, I started studying holistic healing and became a certified herbalist. I read everything I could about how God's creation, plants, minerals, rest, sunlight, can restore us. I prayed over every step of my recovery. I figured if God created it, why not use it to heal me like our ancestors did? I kept choosing life.

And slowly, I came back to life.

I also began learning what true beauty meant. My appearance had changed. My body had changed. But God showed me that beauty is not our hair, our face, or our style. It's our soul. It's the faith we carry when everything else is stripped away.

This journey also opened my eyes to how poorly people with disabilities are treated. I was shocked. I saw firsthand the glares, the impatience, the isolation. I realized how many people live in silence with pain no one else can see. It changed me. I now carry a fire inside me to advocate for those who feel unseen.

Turning Pain into Purpose

By the grace of God, I survived. I'm one of the lucky ones. I still live with side effects, like my right hand or foot giving out, but I know how rare my healing is. I've since started sharing my testimony publicly and have had the honor of speaking to women all over the country. I've brought others to Christ through this journey, not because I had it all together, but because I didn't.

Through the storm, I found my voice. Through the trauma, I found my calling.

Today, I'm working on a book called *When Faith Is All You Have Left*. I want to keep showing people what healing can look like, spiritually, emotionally, and even physically. To spread more awareness about brain tumors.

My scars have become my story. My pain has become my platform.

And I'm not done yet.

A Call to Hope

Before I close, I want to share a word for anyone who feels as though they're still in their valley. If you're walking through a diagnosis, grief, a broken relationship, or a dream that feels out of reach, please hear this: your story isn't over.

There is no valley so deep that God cannot reach you. The same God who met me in an ICU bed, who carried me through nights of pain, uncertainty, and fear, is with you right now. You don't have to have it all figured out; you just need to reach out your hand and trust Him to hold it.

Some days will feel dark and heavy, but the darkness does not get the final word. Hope does. Healing may not look exactly as you expect, but there is purpose in your pain.

Hold fast to the promise of Psalm 34:18: *"The Lord is close to the brokenhearted and saves those who are crushed in spirit."*

I'm living proof that even in the most broken places, God is still writing a beautiful story. And if He did it for me, He can do it for you.

This essay is a snippet of a story I'll be detailing in my upcoming book, which I'm excited to share with the world. Connect with me on Instagram, TikTok, and YouTube (@celena__nichole) to learn more about my journey and my new book!

About Celena

Celena Adams is a two-time brain tumor survivor, Christian public speaker, YouTuber, and author. She is known for her vulnerable storytelling and has inspired thousands through her healing journey and powerful testimony of God's faithfulness.

Just three weeks after marrying the love of her life, Celena was rushed into emergency brain surgery after experiencing stroke-like symptoms. The tumor had overtaken the entire left side of her brain. Uninsured and recently laid off from her executive job, Celena chose to worship through the unknown. Her favorite Scripture, Proverbs 3:5-6, became her lifeline: *"Trust in the Lord with all your heart, and lean not on your own understanding. In all your ways acknowledge him, and he will make straight your paths."*

After the surgery, Celena had to relearn how to walk, speak clearly, and eat again. She lost ten pounds and shaved off the rest of her hair, an act she describes as both painful and liberating. Her husband, Justin, was by her side every step of the way, encouraging her with compassion, hope, and unwavering faith.

Celena now shares her story through public speaking, writing, and ministry. She continues to live with some side effects but considers herself one of the lucky ones. Through it all, she has brought countless people closer to God and continues to use her platform to share awareness, hope, healing, and truth.

She believes this is just the beginning, and her testimony is far from over.

Slaying Orlando

Alyce Bartolomeo

Volunteering has always been a part of my life. From a young age, I watched my father devote his time to others—whether it was fundraising at his church, helping at his Elks Club, or simply stepping in wherever someone needed a hand. He used to tell me that one small act could make a huge difference in someone's life. He always emphasized that when we help others, it should be selfless—not for recognition, not to feel good about ourselves, but simply because it's the right thing to do.

As a child, I listened closely and often helped him with his volunteer work. But it wasn't until I was older that I fully realized how true his words were. The smallest gestures often make the biggest impact.

I carried those lessons with me into adulthood, volunteering for charities whenever I could. But it wasn't until 2012, when my husband Frank was diagnosed with cancer, that I decided to dedicate as much time as possible to helping others.

Frank's battle lasted eleven months. Most of that time was spent in the hospital, through chemo, infections, and bone marrow transplants. I was balancing caring for two children with work, all while staying by his side every night. I'd sleep at the hospital, wash his sheets at home because he hated the hospital ones, and squeeze in thirty minutes on the treadmill just to clear my head—or sometimes just to scream.

I realized how fortunate we were. I could work remotely. We lived close to the hospital. We had friends to help us—one even took care of our dog for those eleven months. We were financially secure and had good insurance. Many families on Frank's hospital floor weren't as lucky. Some patients spent the week completely alone because their loved ones had to work; others struggled just to afford meals or laundry.

So, I tried to help in small ways. I'd pick up groceries for other families, offer to do laundry, or simply stop by patients' doors to chat—fully masked and covered, since infection was always a risk. I kept thinking: We're all going through hell here, but at least I have support. What about the ones who don't?

Back then, there was no Uber, DoorDash, or grocery delivery. Families had so few options. When I asked nurses or hospital staff what resources existed, the answer was always the same: none. I promised myself that when it was all over, I would do something to make life easier for people in those situations.

The financial strain was shocking, too. Every hospital admission cost us a five hundred dollars co-pay. Medications, like the three-hundred-dollar prescription Frank needed after chemo, could cost hundreds of dollars out of pocket unless he was an inpatient. I kept thinking: *How do people survive this?* Not because they're lazy or unwilling to work, but because circumstances beyond their control bury them in bills and stress.

After Frank passed, I joined a fundraiser called Light the Night and raised a decent amount of money. But when I asked where the funds went, no one could give me a clear answer. That didn't sit right with me. I wanted to know if my efforts directly helped people in my community.

So, I tried. I contacted our hospital, asking if I could fund a laundry facility for long-term families. No one could make it happen. I proposed a grocery delivery program for patients without family nearby. Again, I hit red tape and dead ends. It was frustrating.

That's when I shifted my focus. I began fundraising within my community, supporting local families directly and working with charities that could show exactly where the money was going.

I hear my father's words often—*I don't do this to feel good or to brag. I do it so someone else's struggle can be a little lighter.*

For me, philanthropy is about living with purpose, and it's also a way to channel grief and stress into something positive. When you help others, you discover the strength you didn't know you had. Acts of giving connect you to people and allow you to pass down values to your family. Every family we help with is a tribute to Frank. It's about becoming a person who is more compassionate, grateful, and connected.

Every Christmas, my daughter sponsors a family in need. We get their lists of the children's wishes, and there are usually a few modest requests for the parents. Every year, we cry when we see the parents ask for socks or underwear, the most basic necessities. It's a powerful reminder of how lucky we are, and how much need exists right in front of us.

Through all of this, I've learned the point of life isn't to accumulate things, but to show compassion, to be kind, and to make each other's burdens a little lighter. That's the lesson my father taught me. That's the lesson my husband's illness reinforced. And that's the mission I try to live every day.

About Alyce

Alyce Bartolomeo is a serial entrepreneur with a remarkable talent for identifying successful and trending business opportunities. She established many prosperous businesses in her hometown of Westchester, New York, and continued her entrepreneurial endeavors after relocating to Florida.

Philanthropy and volunteering are integral parts of Alyce's life. She has actively served as a PTA president, a Boy Scout/Girl Scout leader, and a member of numerous charity committees. Her profound dedication to helping others is widely recognized, and she is known for her enthusiastic and unhesitating commitment to causes, embodying the principle that "no" is not in her vocabulary.

Alyce is a mother to two children, Mitchell and Allyson, and a grandmother to Mila. In her leisure time, she enjoys traveling with her boyfriend Joe, playing trivia, and hiking. She currently lives in Winter Park, Fla., with her Boston terrier, Bubbles.

One Step Further

Katie Bean

The fourth time I had boarded a plane bound for America, everything was different. There would be no return ticket, no packed suitcases going home. I was sixteen, leaving behind a lifetime in England. I carried anger at my parents for uprooting me, heartbreak over a first love left behind, and the hollow ache of walking away from friends I had known since birth.

As the plane descended into Florida, the heat crashed into me, heavy, unyielding, and mirroring the turmoil I carried inside. Who would I become here? Would I cling to the girl I had been, or step into someone new? I didn't know it then, but that day marked not just an international move. It was the beginning of a story about vision, hospitality, positivity, resilience, connection.

It was about learning, again and again, and taking life one step further.

Vision

My father is a dreamer with unstoppable optimism. Long before we set foot in America, he painted vivid pictures of the life he longed for: a house with a pool, convertible cars in the driveway, a trampoline in the yard. To us, it sounded like fantasy, but his vision was so clear it began to feel inevitable. And in the end, it was.

From him, I have learned that vision is not wishful thinking. It is a map. You must see it, believe it, and pursue it with relentless conviction. At twenty-five, that vision gave me the courage to open my own boutique, and later, to build the life I had once pinned to a vision board, the husband I wanted, the home I imagined, and the future I had only dared to dream. Slowly, those images lifted off the board and became my reality. Vision has carried me through new ventures, failures, fresh starts, and leaps of faith into the unknown. Today, it fuels not just me, but also my team. It has become our shared heartbeat.

Hospitality

Some of my earliest memories are of watching my mum throw dinner parties, music blaring, laughter rolling through the house. She has a gift: she makes everyone feel seen, welcome, celebrated. From her, I learned that hospitality is not optional. It is a calling to make every person who crosses your threshold feel at home.

When I opened my boutique, I found myself living her lessons. People may have come in for the clothing, but they left with something more: a glass of wine, music in the background, conversations that stretched long after shopping bags were full. The store was never about belongings. It was about *belonging*.

Today, in luxury travel, those same instincts still guide me. Hospitality lives in the details, remembering a story, adding a thoughtful touch, turning an arrival into a "Welcome home."

It is the warm hug wrapped around every email, every phone call, and every experience, the care stitched into every itinerary. Hospitality is not just a part of what we do; it is the heart of it all.

Positivity

At nineteen, my sister handed me a copy of *The Four Agreements* by Don Miguel Ruiz. Within minutes, the words felt like they had been waiting for me: do not take things personally, be impeccable with your word, do not make assumptions, always do your best. Suddenly, the noise of judgment and worry faded. I was free to live with intention.

By twenty-five, yet another shift arrived. My best friend dragged me to my first yoga class. I remember the heat, the sweat, and the voice in my head saying, "This is impossible." But yoga taught me to breathe through everything, to soften instead of resist, to keep going. "How you show up on the mat is how you show up in life," they said.

I began whispering mantras, "You can do hard things. Yes, you can." Over time, they became the soundtrack of my life. I learned that the mind believes what you tell it. Seek beauty and the world glows. Seek the negative, and shadows multiply. Again and again, I chose beauty and positivity.

That choice, those breaths, and that knowing, carried me through labor with my two beautiful children, through the heartbreak of closing the doors of my first business, through difficult clients, and through fresh beginnings. Positivity became more than an attitude. It became my compass.

Resilience

I was never a runner, but when a friend invited me to join the New York Marathon, I didn't hesitate. Training was brutal, but by November, I was standing in Staten Island, nerves rattling as the race began.

By mile seventeen, I felt unstoppable. My dad called me mid-stride, and I answered, laughing and breathless, running my fastest mile. But the final mile brought me to the edge of quitting. My legs turned to stone, every step screamed with pain, and my mind filled with excuses. Then I reminded myself what a privilege it was just to be there. So many would give anything for even one step. I lowered my gaze to the pavement and whispered, *yes you can, yes you can*, until finally, I crossed the finish line.

That race became my metaphor for life. Dream big, then move towards that dream, one small step at a time. Positivity is not pretending life is perfect, and resilience is not about never falling. It is finding the strength to rise when everything in you wants to stop.

Connection

When I arrived in America, connection was not optional; it was survival. I had to learn how to walk into rooms where I knew no one, to build belonging from nothing. Over time, that necessity became my strength. When you are truly connected to people, to place, to community, anything is possible.

Connection is the bridge between transaction and transformation. It is at the heart of my work in luxury travel. A trip is never just a trip. It is a chance to weave memories, deepen bonds, and tell stories that last for generations.

At Katie Bean Travels, connection has created more than a business. It has created a home. Clients feel cared for and understood. My team feels safe showing up as themselves, valued for what they bring. Connection is not just what I do. It is who I am. And in every relationship, I try to go one step further: to listen more deeply, to care more fully, to build something that lasts.

Inspiration

In the fall of 2022, I took a trip to Miraval with my best friend. We went looking for yoga and a little girl time and left completely transformed. Those three days gave me a mirror I did not know I needed. The constant lists, the noise, and the responsibilities all quieted, and for the first time in a long while, I could hear myself again. I learned so much about who I was beneath the titles and the to-dos, and I knew more women needed this experience.

When I returned home, I started Mindful Retreats by KBT. Because if just three days of slowing down could shift my perspective so profoundly, imagine what it could do for other women carrying that same weight.

The truth is, as women, we are often conditioned to pour endlessly into others while leaving ourselves empty. We tell ourselves that worth is found in productivity, that rest is indulgence, that showing up for ourselves is somehow selfish. Why would I deserve time for yoga, for reflection, for quiet, when everyone else needs me?

But what Miraval showed me, and what I now carry into every retreat, is that caring for yourself is not selfish. It is essential. When you give yourself permission to breathe, to restore, to listen inward, you return to your family, your work, and your life stronger, steadier, and more present.

Mindful Retreats was created for sacred pauses, spaces where women can step away from the noise and step back into themselves. They are about giving yourself the same hospitality, connection, and care you so easily give to everyone else. Because when women feel renewed and whole, they do not just change their own lives: they inspire everyone around them to do the same.

Define Your Own Pillars

These pillars, Vision, Hospitality, Positivity, Resilience, Connection, are not abstract ideals. They are lived, tested, and chosen. They are my compass when life moves too fast and my lens for what matters most. And woven through them all is the mantra that guides me: One Step Further. It is the practice of reaching beyond what is expected, not only to create something extraordinary, but to inspire others to do the same.

One more act of generosity. One more thoughtful detail. One more layer of care. That is how the ordinary becomes extraordinary, in business, in relationships, in life.

To every woman reading this, my encouragement is simple. Define your own pillars. Let them steady you when the ground feels shaky and light your way when the path is unclear. Pay attention to the people in your life, because they are often your greatest teachers and mirrors. In everything you do, go one step further. In the end, that is how you build not only success, but a legacy.

About Katie

Katie Bean is a storyteller of resilience and possibility, committed to creating moments that matter. Born in London and guided by an unshakable belief in human connection, she transforms travel into experiences that spark joy, meaning, and lasting memories. As the founder of Katie Bean Travels, a Virtuoso luxury travel agency, Katie leads with positivity and purpose, mentoring her team and clients alike to embrace life with courage, curiosity, and heart.

www.katiebeantravels.com
Instagram: @katiebeantravels & @katiemerriganbean
(personal)

Rewriting My Story: From Brokenness to Building Hope

Ashley Bedford

I wasn't born into an easy path. By the time I was thirteen, life had already felt like a storm; chaotic, unpredictable, and filled with moments that could have broken me. My parents were no longer together, my world had splintered, and I was left searching for a place where I truly belonged. Childhood is supposed to be a season of safety and discovery, but mine was shaped by instability and uncertainty.

There were stretches when I leaned on family friends, navigating choices and environments no child should ever have to face. I was hurting, drifting, and trying to fill the emptiness with anything that felt like stability, making choices that pulled me into places I had no business being. I was young, aching, and desperate to mend the cracks that had already formed.

When I finally went to live with my grandparents, I thought stability might follow. And in some ways, it did. There was a roof over my head, a bed to sleep in, and meals on the table. But even there, the love I craved wasn't given in the way I needed. My grandparents provided structure, yes, but not the kind of fierce, unconditional love that heals a girl's wounds. It was a home, but it didn't feel like home.

At fifteen, when the weight of life felt unbearable, I clung to the one truth I could hold onto: God had me. Even if no one else did, I believed He was holding me in the chaos. That belief became my anchor, the small flame of hope that kept me from giving in to the darkness.

The Move That Changed Everything

At eighteen, I packed up what little I had and moved to Florida. I didn't have much; just determination to survive and a boy who wasn't my husband then, but is now the love of my life. Those early days were gritty, the kind of season that tests everything in you. I rode my bike to two different jobs just to make ends meet. The sun was hot, the roads long, and the exhaustion bone-deep, but there was a fire in me that refused to die.

Every morning I woke up, climbed on that bike, and chose to keep moving forward. I didn't have a car, a savings account, or a safety net. What I had was grit. Looking back now, I see that season as one of the most defining of my life. It taught me that resilience isn't built when things are easy. It's forged in the long rides, the sleepless nights, and the moments when quitting seems easier than continuing.

People like to think your beginnings define you. That if you come from brokenness, you'll stay broken. That if your childhood is fractured, your adulthood will be too. But I am living proof that you can rewrite your story. I am not the product of where I came from. I am the product of what I chose to build.

Faith, Family, and Foundation

God didn't just carry me through those years. He began to shape me into the woman I am today. He gave me resilience, grit, and a heart that refused to settle. And He blessed me with an amazing husband, a man who has walked every high and low with me, and two beautiful daughters who are my greatest treasures. My family is proof that restoration is possible, even when your foundation feels like it's made of sand.

When I look at my girls, I don't just see their smiles. I see redemption. I see answered prayers. I see living proof that cycles can be broken and new legacies can be written. The love I longed for as a child, I get to pour into them every day. And in doing so, God heals pieces of me I didn't even know were still tender.

Finding My Calling

Over time, I discovered my calling: helping families step into stability through homeownership. For some, a house might look like just a set of keys and a mortgage payment. But for me and for the people I serve, it's so much more. It's safety. It's hope. It's the foundation for generational wealth.

As a mortgage broker, I get to guide people through one of the biggest decisions of their lives. But for me, it's not just about loans and rates; it's about rewriting legacies. It's about creating stability where there once was chaos. Every closing I do is another family stepping into a new chapter, just like I did years ago.

I know what it's like to feel like the odds are stacked against you. I know what it's like to wonder if stability will ever be yours. And that's why this work matters so deeply to me. Because when someone gets the keys to their first home, it's not just a house; it's hope. It's the moment they realize their story doesn't have to end the way it began.

Building More Than Business

My journey hasn't just been about business, though. It's been about mission. Today I serve on the boards of And Still She Stands, an organization empowering women to rise from brokenness, and Foster Youth of America, which fights for kids who, like me, know what it feels like to be forgotten.

When I walk into those rooms, I don't just show up as a professional or a leader. I show up as a woman who's lived it. I see myself in every girl who feels unseen, in every child who wonders if they're worth it. And I tell them with my life: Yes, you are.

I remind them that their worth is not defined by where they started. That broken beginnings don't have to mean broken futures. That God can take ashes and turn them into beauty, even when it feels impossible.

Defying the Odds

The truth is, I should not be here. By every statistic, I should have stayed stuck. I should have been another number in the cycle of broken families, absent love, and lost potential. But I didn't. Not because the road was easy, but because I chose to believe that God had something greater for me. Because I chose to fight for the life I wanted, even when it meant pedaling a bike to two jobs in the Florida heat.

And here's the thing: the fight never really ends. Life still throws storms, but now I know how to stand in them. I know how to anchor myself in faith, surround myself with people who pour into me, and keep my eyes fixed on the future instead of the past.

What I've Learned

When people look at me today, they might see a successful businesswoman, a wife, a mom, a community leader. And I am all those things. But underneath it all, I am still that girl who had every reason to give up and didn't.

If there's one thing I want women, young people, and anyone walking through their own storm to know, it's this: You are not a product of your circumstances. You are not a victim. You are the author of your story.

And with faith, grit, and relentless hope, you can rewrite it into something beautiful.

A Message to the Next Generation

To the girl who feels unseen: I see you.

To the boy who feels forgotten: You matter.

To the woman who thinks it's too late: It's not.

To the family who feels like stability is out of reach: It's closer than you think.

Your story isn't finished. Your beginning does not dictate your ending. And the storm you're standing in today might just be the soil where God is planting the seeds of your future.

Choose Your Own Ending

My journey has been long, messy, and far from perfect. But it has also been redemptive, purposeful, and overflowing with grace. And if my story can do anything, I hope it reminds others that no matter where you start, you have the power to choose a different ending.

You can rise from brokenness.

You can break cycles.

You can build legacies.

And you can live a life that not only blesses you, but blesses generations to come.

Because if God could take a hurting thirteen-year-old girl, anchor her in hope, and transform her into the woman I am today. He can do it for anyone.

About Ashley

Ashley Bedford, affectionately known as The Mortgage Magician, is a nationally recognized mortgage broker with Appli Home Loans. Her journey is one of faith, resilience, and transformation—proof that no matter the storms, still she stands.

Ashley brings that same strength into her career, helping families move beyond the fear of numbers to find confidence in homeownership. To her, a mortgage is more than a loan; it's a key to stability, healing, and building generational wealth.

Deeply rooted in service, Ashley also serves on the boards of And Still She Stands and Foster Youth of America, using her story and platform to empower women and youth to rise, rebuild, and thrive.

Away from work, Ashley is a proud wife, as well as a mom to two beautiful daughters and corgi fur babies. Family, faith, and community remain the heart of who she is and the reason she continues to stand strong for herself, her clients, and her community.

The Strength of Scars: from Chaos to Purpose

Katherine Carpio

That day, sitting in my closet with that thought whispering, *Do it, nothing matters anymore,* was the first time I experienced suicidal thoughts, unthinkable for someone raised in the Catholic faith. I remember walking out, sitting in the backyard for hours, praying and begging for strength, the kind I no longer felt I had by my own will. Some describe it as hitting rock bottom. For me, it was simply knowing that what I felt that day was something I never wanted to feel again. That day, I understood something: my mind could lie to me, but my faith would never abandon me.

I was born and raised in Venezuela, a country where its leaders fail its people. I'm the oldest of two sisters. My sister was one of God's first signs that I was special to Him.

He sent her to me as a gift on my fifth birthday; twenty-one years later, He would also give me my first daughter as a birthday gift. Yes, I'm still trying to figure out what it means that the three of us were all born on the same day.

My parents worked hard to build a life full of opportunities and abundance for us. They showed me that honest work, and especially teamwork, could build big companies and prosperous lives. They became one of the five largest distributors in their field in the country, and with that came my responsibility as the eldest: by the time I was eighteen, I was learning to manage a company I would later inherit.

I studied and graduated as a CPA, and that's where my first years as a businesswoman began. Between managing daily operations, making sure orders were delivered on time, and attending meetings with bank executives, I was learning how to lead. At home, they were my parents, but in the office, they were my bosses, and they treated me as such. That shaped my character and taught me responsibility—lessons that would later help me manage my own companies and lead a team of real estate agents.

But when an entire life perfectly planned and mapped out gets ripped from you in a single breath, you have no choice. Forced to leave my country overnight after an attempted kidnapping, with a baby in my arms and fear weighing on my chest, I remember walking to the airplane door drenched in tears, out of breath, holding a ticket that read Orlando, Fla.

Sometimes the ticket that hurts the most is the same one that takes you to the place where you'll rebuild your life. Ten years later, this city has become the home of my greatest achievements, but also my deepest disappointments, pains, and losses.

December 18, 2019, is a morning I'll never forget. That was the day my world came to a complete stop. In a cold doctor's office, the doctor looked at me with compassion, carrying the responsibility of telling a mother that her world was about to become darker and harder.

That same morning, before leaving the house, I stood in front of the stove. My mother's heart already knew. In an act of surrender, I prayed and asked God to walk with me, because I had no idea how I was going to handle it. When I flipped the bread, a cross had burned onto it. It felt like God had opened a direct channel with me. That's when I confirmed that when you don't have human answers, God gives you divine signs.

Back in the doctor's office, I experienced something I would only learn years later had a name: depersonalization. It's the feeling of being separated from your own body, like an outside observer of yourself and what's happening in the moment. It's usually triggered by trauma or extreme stress.

Then I heard the words, "Autism, level II. Mom, your only responsibility is to help her speak before she turns five." And that's what the next three years of my life became.

I gave myself completely, body and soul, to making Ana speak. She was two and a half at the time. Long, exhausting days trying to understand behaviors typical of autism. Nights spent searching YouTube, books, podcasts, social media, anything that could help me learn, understand, and face this new world that had now become my life. All while trying to balance being a wife, a businesswoman, and a mom to my seven-year-old daughter, Karla.

I don't need to say much for you to picture it: it was chaos. I wasn't working. I spent my days inside four walls, my only conversations with a three-year-old who couldn't answer me. Toys piled up in the living room. Breakfast dishes still sat on the table at six p.m. And me, still in pajamas, staring at it all with a mix of guilt and exhaustion. Today I know: those scenes weren't a failure. They were the training ground preparing me for everything that was to come.

Day by day, life with Ana became a little more manageable. I had to remember the saying, something like, *Where you place your attention, you place your energy, and it grows.* I had to help her speak before she turned five. Long story short: she did. At four and a half, she said it: "Mom." And from there, everything changed.

That's life: a small win in the middle of chaos, just enough to give you a breath and keep you going.

We were in the middle of the pandemic. Our business had collapsed, and suddenly the four of us were locked in a house that had only "worked" until then because we spent most of the day apart.

My relationship with my then-husband grew increasingly tense. And my oldest daughter also began to feel the constant pressure. It broke me to feel like I was losing precious moments with her; between the fights at home and her sister's meltdowns, our calm and our bond were slipping away.

But right there, I discovered something I'll never forget: Karla, my oldest daughter, is pure courage. She's not afraid to say what she thinks, even when her voice is uncomfortable. She is the version of me I always wanted to be when I was growing up, but never dared.

From her, I learned persistence. From her, I learned that speaking your truth is also an act of love. And I understood that, even when I was falling apart, she reminded me of the woman I could be.

Today, I know my daughters have been my pillars. Ana taught me resilience, patience, empathy, and that there is always another way to do things and that it's okay. Those abilities prepare you to manage teams with multiple personalities, to see each person for who they are and what they can contribute if they're given the space and support they need. And her older sister taught me courage and authenticity. They are the reason I never stayed down.

And so, without realizing it, a leader was being formed in me, one who would be tested in many ways later. At the end of the day, only a few of us dare to step out of the pattern and fight for what we consider to be our happiness. Mine, if you ask me, is to live my days on my own terms. To be where I want, not where I "should be." To be present in my daughters' lives and surrounded by people who make me better in every way.

My journey of rebuilding was only beginning. During that time, I came face-to-face with depression and suicidal thoughts, but I also met a woman who would leave an unforgettable mark on me: Angélica Behm. Although God only gave us a few months together, they were enough to mark a before and after in me.

By then, I had been licensed in real estate for two years and had already gone through two brokerages where nothing seemed to work. But Angélica saw me differently. She didn't look at me for what I was in that moment; she looked at me for what I could become.

Sometimes we need someone to lend us their eyes when ours can no longer see our worth. That's what she did for me, and for many other women in the industry.

In real estate, there's a saying I've always hated: "You're only as good as your last deal."

I hate it, because it's not true.

Behind every closing there are dozens of attempts, most ending in a no. There are nights of tears, of comparing your progress with others, of asking yourself if you're good enough.

What no one tells you is that those no's are the ones that build you. That real growth doesn't happen at the closing table; it happens in the invisible process no one claps for.

That's where I learned something that changed my career: Success in real estate isn't about chasing clients. It's about attracting opportunities from your essence.

Essence, that word that often feels abstract and hard to define. Your personal brand reflects who you really are: in the way you dress, in every email you send, in every post you share. Because you stop trying to fit in and start to resonate. And if there's one thing I want you to take from these lines, something you can apply or at least let spark your curiosity today, it's this: "Build your personal brand." It's not about likes; it's not about followers. That's not the way.

Abundance can't be copied. It shows up when you've done the inner work.

When your essence leads, success stops being a chase and becomes attraction. That's when opportunities find you. And it feels like there was no other way, only God answering prayers.

Something that has always moved me is helping my people. In every step I take and every direction I go, and in my career, it couldn't be any different. After living firsthand how my parents were scammed and lost much of the wealth they had built by putting their money in the wrong place, it became crystal clear to me: I had to work with my Latino community, helping them identify real investment opportunities.

Along the way, I've been able to walk alongside dozens of families to help them achieve their goals, but I also discovered something that fills my soul even more than my pockets: helping other real estate agents solidly grow their careers.

And with that comes a world of challenges: envy, jealousy, betrayal, some of the lowest things. I've had to live them, heal, and choose to leave them behind to follow my dream. The purpose God has for me is to impact thousands of lives through my story.

Because I:

- Choose to act from the heart.
- Choose to give what I truly carry inside.
- Choose not to give by inertia, but with purpose.

Because I believe in a world where honesty, transparency, inclusion, and empathy are true freedom and the bridge that brings us closer to God. I learned that my scars are not my shame; they are proof that God used me to write a story bigger than myself.

My scars don't limit me. They are the language God chose to write my purpose.

Today, I know my life isn't measured in closed transactions, but in lives touched and the faith that sustains me. Success that truly transcends isn't measured in numbers, but in the lives you transform along the way.

If the past taught me anything, it's that God never wastes pain; each wound shaped the woman I am destined to be. My faith, my heart, and my daughters kept me standing even in the darkest days. Today I can say with certainty that I'm not here because of what I sold, but because of what I built with faith, clarity, and heart. And if my story can remind you of something, it's this: your pain may mark you, but only your purpose can define you.

About Katherine

Katherine Carpio is a Florida real estate investment advisor who has transformed her personal story into a powerful professional mission. After overcoming seasons of chaos and rebuilding her life from the ground up, she turned every challenge into an opportunity. Today, she guides international families and investors in protecting their capital and building lasting wealth in the United States.

With over a decade of experience, Katherine has become an influential voice in Florida's pre-construction and short-term rental markets, especially in Miami and Orlando. Her work goes beyond numbers—it is about the human impact behind each decision: a family's dream, the security of a future, the vision of a legacy.

In addition to serving clients, Katherine is a mentor to other real estate agents, empowering them to sell with authenticity, confidence, and strategy. She firmly believes that true professional success is born from personal scars and that leading with heart is the key to making a lasting impact.

Today, Katherine combines her expertise, resilience, and magnetic energy to inspire others to dare for more—not only to build properties, but also to build stories of success and transformation.

Istagram: @katherinecarpiorealtor
Facebook: https://www.facebook.com/kathycarpiorealtor
LinkedIn: https://www.linkedin.com/in/katherine-carpio-realtor
YouTube: https://www.youtube.com/@katherinecarpiorealtor
www.katherinecarpiorealtor.com

Two Oaths, One Purpose: How I Became a Healer, a Citizen, and the Architect of a Life I Once Only Imagined

Dr. Elizabeta Cokovska

It was a quiet morning, the kind I love most, with a perfectly hot cup of coffee in my hands and a good conversation flowing with a friend. Somewhere between laughter and reflection, something struck me: how success, once achieved, starts to feel ordinary. We reach milestones we once dreamed about, only to find ourselves looking forward again, planning, striving, wondering what's next. You don't always stop to realize how far you've actually come. I smiled into my coffee that morning because when I paused long enough to reflect, I saw a story, *my* story: one that's filled with determination, resilience, and the quiet power of never taking "no" for an answer.

I've always known who I was, even at a very young age. I was almost six years old when I first learned what it meant to believe in myself, even when others didn't. I wanted to start school, and I still remember overhearing my teacher tell my father that I wasn't ready for school and the mix of fear and determination I felt as I listened. But my father disagreed. He stood up for me, looked that teacher in the eye, and said that I *was* ready and that I could do it. And just like that, I started school, exactly as I wanted. Looking back, that moment planted a seed in me, that sometimes the world won't see your readiness, your potential, or your fire, but you have to hold on to it anyway. That lesson has stayed with me all my life: when others doubt you, you have to believe in yourself twice as hard.

I rose to the top of my class, not because I aimed to simply pass tests, but because I was driven to truly understand the essence of my chosen field. I studied day and night, determined to build a strong foundation for everything I hoped to become. When I graduated from dental school in Europe, I dreamed of becoming a prosthodontist—a specialist focused on restoring smiles and rebuilding confidence. But once again, I was told it wasn't possible. The program was exclusive, reserved for the privileged few. I didn't have that kind of background, but I had something else: drive. I was offered every other specialty, but my heart refused to settle. I wanted prosthodontics or nothing at all. So I kept applying, kept trying, kept believing. I didn't want just any career; I wanted the one I was meant for. And one day, I got in.

That moment didn't just prove that dreams are possible; it proved that determination is stronger than doubt. Every "no" I heard had brought me closer to the one "yes" that mattered.

Not long after that victory, life brought a new challenge that would change my story completely. My husband, an engineer, and I decided to immigrate to the United States. There was a war in our country, and we wanted a safer, better future for our family. We applied through the US embassy and were granted an interview. They say the selection process is random, but deep down, I believe they look for something more: people with strong educational backgrounds and the potential to contribute something meaningful. We had a young daughter and another baby on the way. It was a leap of faith, one of those life-changing decisions where you can't see what's ahead, but you know you have to jump anyway. Then, on one ordinarily beautiful day, we got the news that we were one of the few who had been chosen for a green card.

We came to America with two suitcases, an icon, and only $10,000 in our pockets.

I'll never forget the moment we landed in Florida. The second those airport doors opened, the hot, heavy air hit my face: a wave of warmth that felt almost symbolic, like an embrace from the new world I was stepping into. I didn't know what awaited us, but I knew I was exactly where I needed to be. That moment was over twenty years ago, and yet I can still feel that warm air, that mix of fear and excitement, that quiet whisper in my heart saying, *This is your new beginning*. It was the first moment of the rest of my life.

I was a doctor, but in a new country, that title didn't mean much at first. I was seven months pregnant when I got a job as a dental assistant. My English was limited, but my gratitude was limitless. I'll never forget the doctor who believed in me enough to give me that opportunity. That kind of faith, someone taking a chance on you, can change the entire course of your life. My family didn't have much, but we had each other, and that made us rich in all the ways that truly matter. Happiness, I learned, doesn't come from comfort; it comes from gratitude. We were grateful for every meal, every moment, and every opportunity.

I worked hard, step by step, from dental assistant to dental hygienist, but deep down in my soul I knew I wasn't done. My heart longed for prosthodontics, the specialty that had defined my purpose. Dentistry wasn't just my career; it was my passion. I loved restoring not just teeth, but confidence, identity, and joy. I wanted to help people smile again, not just on the outside, but from the inside out. So, I did something most people thought was impossible: I went back to school again, this time in the United States, to earn my credentials all over and reclaim my title as a prosthodontist here.

There were days when exhaustion felt endless. But every challenge reminded me of something my journey had already taught me: that nothing is impossible when your purpose is bigger than your struggle. My passion and faith were too big to be silenced by fear or fatigue.

Through the never-ending help and support of my wonderful husband and children, I achieved my goal and began practicing again. Working for other dental offices helped me gain experience and refine my skills. I soon realized that I no longer wanted to work for anyone else, and a quiet voice inside of me began to whisper again: *It's time to build your own.* I realized I was ready to create something of my own that reflected my vision, my values, and my dedication to my patients.

That's how *Makris Dental Prosthodontics* was born.

The name "Makris" is special. It's a combination of my daughters' names, a tribute to the two people who motivated me through every obstacle. They were my reason, my inspiration, and my reminder that dreams are worth chasing. Building my own practice was more than a career move; it was the realization of a dream I had nurtured for decades.

I spent months searching for the right location, driving around Florida, walking empty plots of land, and trying to imagine where my dream would take root. When I stepped foot on the land in Lake Nona, located in the heart of Orlando's Medical City, I knew instantly it was the right spot. It felt alive and full of innovation, growth, and hope. Florida had welcomed me when I arrived with nothing, and now, it was the place where I would plant new roots and give back to the community that gave me so much. I designed and built my practice from the ground up, every wall and every detail filled with my vision and passion.

Every time I walk through the doors of my practice, I feel immense gratitude for my patients, my team, and the life that I've built. I get to do what I love every single day and live my dream to restore smiles, rebuild confidence, and make a difference in people's lives. That's not just my job; it's my calling. What fulfills me most isn't the success itself; it's the journey that made it possible. It's knowing that no matter where you start, you can build the life you envision if you have the courage to keep going. Success, I've learned, isn't just about achievements or titles. It's about impact. It's about the people you help, the moments you share, and the legacy you build.

If there's one lesson my story carries, it's this: *never let anyone define what's possible for you.* People will tell you no. Life will test you. But if you know who you are and what you want, you'll always find a way. Success doesn't happen overnight; it's built day by day, through persistence, passion, and purpose.

In my life, I have taken two oaths, the Hippocratic Oath and the Oath of Allegiance: one to serve humanity, and one to serve the nation that gave me the freedom to do so. Together, they define not just my profession, but my soul.

No matter where you come from, no matter how many times you've heard "no," there's always a "yes" waiting for you, but you have to believe you're worthy of finding it. That's what my journey taught me. That's what becoming an American, and a specialist prosthodontist living my dream, has reminded me every single day. Because sometimes, the most beautiful part of success isn't reaching the destination. It's realizing that you made it ... all the way home.

About Elizabeta

Dr. Elizabeta Cokovska is a distinguished master specialist prosthodontist, visionary leader, and founder of Makris Dental Prosthodontics, an elite dental practice located in Lake Nona, the vibrant heart of Orlando's renowned Medical City. With over thirty years of experience, she has built a reputation as one of the most accomplished and compassionate professionals in restorative and aesthetic dentistry.

Dr. Cokovska holds two prosthodontic specialties and two master's degrees in her field, an achievement that reflects her unwavering commitment to excellence to her profession. She began her career in Europe, where she completed her first master's degree and specialty in prosthodontics, quickly establishing herself as a leading expert in complex dental rehabilitation. Her pursuit of excellence and innovation led her to the United States, where she was accepted into the prestigious Henry M. Goldman School of Dental Medicine at Boston University, one of the nation's most renowned dental institutions. There, she earned her second master's degree and completed her postdoctoral specialty in prosthodontics, becoming a specialist doctor on two continents.

Driven by passion and guided by purpose, Dr. Cokovska's work is a reflection of her lifelong mission: to restore smiles, confidence, and quality of life for every patient she treats. Her practice is known for its uncompromising excellence, cutting-edge technology, and a deeply personalized approach. Her expertise lies in solving the most complex restorative and reconstructive cases, where experience meets precision and passion, and empathy guides every decision. For her, dentistry is more than just a profession: it is her calling.

Instagram: @makrisdentalprosthodontics
Facebook:
https://www.facebook.com/profile.php?id=61579597835777
www.makrisdental.com
contact@makrisdental.com

Who Cares What They Said

Shay Edwards

My name is Shay Edwards. I am a wife and mother of five. I am also a salon owner, business coach, mentor, Ms. Orlando in the Ms. Corporate America 2025 pageant, and an advocate for domestic violence survivors who volunteers with FPEDV and One Heart Women and Children.

I've spent over two decades in the beauty industry, and if you ask me where it really began, I'd have to take you back to my grandmother Martha's house.

I was three years old. I lived with my grandmother as a child, and one warm summer night in 1988, Grandma decided to have a sleepover at her house. The house was full with all my cousins, lots of laughter, and games. Everyone was caught up in a board game, but my eyes were glued to something else—my older cousin braiding her baby doll's hair.

I remember the excitement that filled me as I watched. I asked, "How do you do that?" She showed me once more, and with my tiny hands, I tried it. Astonished that I actually made a braid, the room was filled with celebration. I had no idea that tiny moment was planting a seed that would grow into my life's purpose.

By kindergarten, I was already hooked. When my Aunt Rena interviewed me for a kids' newsletter, she asked, "What do you want to be when you grow up?" Without hesitation, I said, "A hairdresser." She smiled and corrected me, "You mean a cosmetologist?" I nodded. That article is still with me today, proof that I always knew who I was meant to be.

Throughout my childhood, I practiced on dolls, my little sister, and eventually the neighborhood kids. By age twelve, I was charging just twenty-five dollars for styles that took hours. I wasn't thinking about overhead or business expenses; I was just thrilled someone trusted me with their head and put cash in my hand. Those years taught me more than how to do hair. They taught me patience, people skills, and the joy of creating beauty out of nothing.

At sixteen, I had this crazy idea that I boldly told my clients, "I want to retire by the time I am fifty years old." What I meant by that statement is that all the hard grinding that I saw many adults in my life doing, I didn't want to do forever. I always wanted to travel and be in good health when I did retire. Even though I rarely left Orlando, Fla., and the thought of boarding an airplane was outlandish, I wanted year fifty to be the point in my life where I worked because I loved what I did and not because I needed to just pay bills. Some encouraged me to speak it into existence. Others, especially family, said, "Girl, be realistic. Get your head out of the clouds." That tension between faith in my dreams and fear of disappointment followed me for years.

After high school, I was supposed to continue college with a scholarship. When that fell through, I had to pivot. I chose cosmetology school instead. I loved every moment of those nine months, but reality hit hard once I entered the salon world. I rented a booth, tried to pay weekly rent, but I didn't have enough clients and income to cover the cost. Within weeks, I was behind in my rent. I remember the shame of realizing, "I can't make this work right now." I packed up and went back home, uncertain of what came next.

I went back to school for business, determined to build a different future, but life happened. I had to move out on my own at nineteen, and bills piled up on me. I had to work two jobs in order to cover my bills. I withdrew from school because I missed class due to my work schedule, thinking it would just be temporary. That break lasted seven years.

In those years, I got married—twice—and had three children. Eventually, I was raising them on my own. I kept doing hair on the side, but most of my energy went to survival. I worked corporate jobs because they paid the bills. While hair remained a passion, I couldn't figure out how to make it sustainable.

By 2015, I was juggling it all: full-time work, raising three kids, college coursework, and clients at night. My routine was brutal. Up at six thirty a.m., school drop-offs, eight hours at work, hair until midnight, then papers until 3 or 4 a.m. My body ran on coffee and Red Bull. I did this for four straight years.

And then I broke.

My body shut down. I ended up in the ER, in pain so bad I could feel blood moving through my veins. The doctors couldn't find anything. They sent me home with naproxen. But I knew something was deeply wrong. At the same time, I received a letter: my landlord was selling the condo, and I had thirty days to vacate.

I was sick, I was homeless, and I was scared. I began to read Matthew 6:25-24 and Philippians 4:13.

I kept telling myself, "God is always faithful, and he never fails." Then I received a call from a sister from church who had a friend with a vacancy. "Praise the Lord!!" I found a small one-bedroom apartment. It wasn't much, but it gave us shelter and time to heal. I quit caffeine and energy drinks cold turkey. For the first time in years, I only worked the well-paying corporate job I just landed, and came home each day, with no extra obligations or pressure. Slowly, I rebuilt my strength. I learned a hard truth: if I didn't create balance, I wouldn't be here for my kids or my clients.

When I graduated college in 2016, my mindset shifted. I realized I couldn't keep treating my gift like a hobby. Hair was a business. By 2017, I began studying, attending classes, raising my prices, and using an online booking system. I built clientele at home. After building a steady flow, I moved into a salon chair and then two chairs with an assistant.

After seeing my dreams start to form, I got thirsty for knowledge. I read everything I could. One day, while working in insurance sales, my manager gave me Napoleon Hill's *Think and Grow Rich*. I devoured it in two weeks. That book lit a fire in me. All my life, I'd been told my dreams were unrealistic. That book said the opposite: whatever you can imagine, you can create. Around the same time, I discovered *The Secret* on Netflix. I watched it every week for months, learning how to shift my energy, thoughts, and vision.

I started writing a list of my goals. Then I built a vision board. Within two years, everything on it came true. I had to make a new one. That taught me the power of mindset, faith, and speaking life over myself.

By 2022, I opened my salon suite, Boss Up Braiding.

I'll never forget walking into that suite for the first time. The smell of Ashtae products filled the air. The chairs were lined up, the tools ready. For the first time in decades, I felt the weight lift. I could breathe. I had built something sustainable, not just for me, but for my children and for the women I would employ and mentor.

But my biggest transformation wasn't just in business; it was in my mind. As Proverbs 23:7 says, "As a man thinketh in his heart, so is he." I realized that I am not merely the product of circumstances and situations; I am a reflection of how I see myself. How I see myself gives me permission to dream as big as I want to.

Today, I am living proof that no dream is too big. From doing twenty-five-dollar braids standing outside on people's back porches in middle school to owning Boss Up Braiding Salon, educating globally, coaching and mentoring stylists, serving as Ms. Orlando (MCA), magazine contributor, speaker, and *Slaying Orlando* author, my life is a testimony that is still being written.

Every day, when I stand behind my chair or in front of a classroom, I remember the three-year-old girl who was nestled under her cousin's arm, learning her first braid. That girl had no idea how hard the road would be. But she also had no idea how strong she would become.

I also see the single mother who often cried on the way to work many days, exhausted, wondering how I would afford to keep the lights on and still be present for my children. I see the woman who felt torn between chasing her dreams and raising her family. What I've learned is this: you don't have to choose. You can have both.

You can build a thriving business and still show up for the people you love.

That's why I created the Bossuprenuer Coaching Program to show entrepreneurs how to build six-figure businesses, reclaim their time, and stop shrinking their dreams. Because the truth is, when women step fully into their gifts, they don't just change their own lives, they change generations.

If you're reading this and wondering how to start creating balance, here are two things that changed my life:

1. Plan family time and work time separately. Put them both on the calendar with equal weight. When I'm with family, I'm fully present. When I'm working, I give it my all.
2. Take time for yourself. Even if it's just thirty minutes a week, step away from everyone and everything. Breathe, pray, journal, or sit in silence. My peace fuels my purpose.

My message to you is simple: Don't shrink your dreams. Protect them, nurture them, and chase them with everything you have. Anything you imagine can be your reality with faith, vision, and perseverance.

If a little girl who was told her head was in the clouds and her dreams were too big can build a business, empower women, and change lives—then so can you.

About Shay

Shay Edwards is an accomplished salon owner, business coach, mentor, educator, and philanthropist with over twenty-two years of professional experience in the beauty industry. She is the CEO of *Boss Up Braiding*, a premier braiding and natural hair salon, and the founder of the *Bossuprenuer Coaching*

Program, where she equips beauty professionals with the systems and strategies to scale into six-figure success.

As an educator for *Ashtae Products*, Shay has trained and mentored stylists across the country, blending artistry with entrepreneurship. She also holds a bachelor's in business administration and a minor in human resources and is a licensed insurance agent specializing in life and health services, giving her a unique perspective on business growth, leadership, and financial empowerment.

Shay is also an accomplished writer and speaker. She is a contributing author in the anthology *Slaying Orlando* and a contributor to *AHP Indie Stylist Magazine*. She has also spoken on panels, podcasts, and major stages, and has hosted live events where she inspires and educates audiences on leadership, business, and personal growth.

Crowned Ms. Orlando in the *Ms. Corporate America* 2025 competition, Shay uses her platform to advocate for women and families, with a special focus on supporting survivors of domestic violence. She is also an active member of *Florida Partners to End Domestic Violence*, bringing awareness and resources to beauty professionals. Her philanthropic work is an extension of her mission to create impact beyond beauty.

With a portfolio that spans beauty, business, education, writing, and community leadership, Shay Edwards continues to inspire others to dream bigger, work smarter, and lead with purpose.

My Story

Cathy McCaw Engelman

Life is a journey, and with each decade or so, another chapter unfolds. My journey began at St. Mary Magdalene, Bishop Moore High School, and then Belmont Abbey College, where I was educated by the Benedictine monks. My years at Belmont Abbey allowed me not only to learn from a monastic community, but also to socialize and interact with this religious order. I was profoundly influenced by the monks; I admired their lives and their selfless concern for their students and community.

I was raised in a large Catholic family with four siblings. My parents were selfless and sacrificed to put us all through private schools and five different colleges. Growing up in a household of seven, I remember vividly talking with my parents about college and what I wanted to do when I graduated. I always wanted to go into interior design or fashion. Both of my parents had incredible taste. They were both from New York City (NYC), where my father worked for Schumacher selling fabrics and wallpaper, and my mother worked in the garment exchange. I got my love of design from them both.

When I announced to them that I wanted to go to Parsons School of Design, I was first met with silence, then they both said "no." In 1981, NYC wasn't a very safe place, and there were no internships with people like Ralph Lauren, Tory Burch, or Zimmerman. Although times have since changed, opportunities for me to pursue design were limited back then. I remember feeling very disappointed, but also grateful that my parents had the money to send me out of state. I ended up pivoting, and my father pushed me to think about healthcare or medicine.

I ended up going to Belmont Abbey College in North Carolina. I majored in biology and, upon graduation, spent twenty-five years in the workers' compensation industry and specializing in home health care, infusion therapy, durable medical equipment, medical supplies, mail order pharmacy, and prescription benefit management services. I worked as both a sales representative and sales manager. For twenty-four years, I worked in sales, and for fifteen years, I managed a sales force of forty from Florida to Maine.

As you can imagine, there was extensive travel involved, and I often did sixty- or seventy-hour work weeks. While on maternity leave with my second child, my company announced they were going from four managers to two nationwide. This meant I would basically be handling not only the East Coast, but the whole country. With a three-year-old daughter and a newborn son, I saw the writing on the wall that I was being pushed out—even after glowing reviews and having won Director of the Year the previous month. I was crushed. I took the severance package, but as the old saying goes, "when one door closes, another opens."

A year before this happened, my husband and I had started a national language interpretation and medical transportation company. My salary had kept us afloat and enabled us to maintain our lifestyle while the business was being built. The timing was right, after I got laid off, and I joined him in our business. As CEO, he handled operations and contracts, and as VP of sales, I managed the nationwide sales force and handled the Florida sales as well. Extensive travel was involved, as well as high levels of stress, and I had to focus on balancing my "two" lives—one as a mother of two toddlers, and the other as a business owner and entrepreneur.

My husband and I co-owned that business for nine years. They were good years, working as a team and creating a very successful business. When we traveled, we took my mother and children with us. In 2009, we sold two divisions of our company, and I decided to retire. Around that time, my husband wanted me to look into taking our kids away to Europe for a year and traveling with a tutor. I spoke with the principal at my daughter's school, who recommended taking the trip before my daughter started high school (she was starting seventh grade at the time).

Three months later, my husband came home from work and said he wanted a divorce.

I'm not sure if you have gone through this, but it was a complete shock, and I was completely blindsided. Just when I thought we had really made it and I could focus on spending time with my kids, my world imploded.

Imagine reinventing yourself at forty-six, retired, and raising a twelve-year-old and an eight-year-old. It was a dark time in my life.

Twenty-six years ago, I also lost my father when I was pregnant with my daughter. A few years later, I lost my beautiful and adored sister Beth to colon cancer when she was only fifty-six. Then came the loss of my good friend's thirteen-year-old daughter to a brain tumor, a very public and painful divorce, and the death of my beloved mother to dementia. I share this with you because I was at a crossroads in my life. I was retired, but still raising young children. I was contemplating how to move on to the next chapter. I will tell you, my Catholic faith and the power of prayer helped me tremendously, but so did the support of family and friends.

I share this with you because I was feeling stuck and trying to find a way to move on. I would like to acknowledge a good friend, Jimmy Ferrell, who is not only my financial advisor, but also my spiritual advisor. He once told me, "Keep your eye on God and those two beautiful children, and all will work out." Over lunch one day, he suggested I use my time and talent to step up and start doing more volunteer work. I am sure he didn't realize it at the time, but his kind words and lots of prayers helped me move on to the next chapter, which has been very fulfilling and rewarding.

Over the last twenty years, I have been involved in the following organizations: I'm a dedicated supporter of The Catholic Diocese of Orlando, St. Margaret Mary Catholic School, Bishop Moore High School, and Dr. Phillips Center for the Performing Arts. I'm on the UCF Foundation board and the Council of 101, and I work with the Orlando Museum of Art and Support Our Scholars. I also work with the University of Central Florida College of Medicine, where my children and I donated a cancer research machine in honor of my sister Beth.

In 2019, Tom Doyle, President of Bishop Moore High School, asked me to chair the fundraising for the Moore Center, a new athletic center with boys' and girls' lockers and more dedicated classrooms. In the year leading up to COVID, my team and I were able to raise over four million dollars and make the new building a reality. Bishop Moore later honored my efforts at an eight-hundred-person gala.

While preparing my speech that year, my then nineteen-year-old son asked, "Why do you give?" The mother in me used this as an opportunity to educate him on the importance of giving back and the responsibility he has moving forward. I responded that people give because they want to help. People give because it feels good. People give because of tradition. But most people give because they want to make their community better. I then explained that I choose to give to an organization that I trust and value. I give to an organization that shares my mission. I give to an organization where I have a personal connection, and I give where I can make a difference. In just one year, my team and I were able to make the Moore Center a reality for future generations to enjoy.

I am just completing the finishing touches on a new home in Winter Park. It has been a four-year new-build project. It is full of color, wallpapers, gorgeous textiles, and many incredible details. I even have a pink front door, a pink gate, and pink and white awnings. It's been a true labor of love. Over the last fifteen years, my beautiful children, Madison (age twenty-five) and Ian (age twenty-two), have been after me to do something creative.

My son tells me, "Everywhere we go, people love the way you dress and express yourself." So this year I decided to pursue the dream of designing and creating a line of evening shoes in Italy. My daughter came up with the name Catarina Atelier—the English translation of *catarina* is "pure." My boyfriend Quentin and I just arrived back from Italy and are just starting up the new business. We will launch in 2026 so I have time to do things right.

Pivoting, changing, adjusting, evolving, just like I've done over the last sixteen years. Thank you for reading my story.

About Cathy

Cathy McCaw Engelman is a mother of two beautiful children, former healthcare executive, and retired owner of a national language interpretation and medical transportation company. She's highly organized and driven and was a fearless sales leader for over twenty-five years. These days, you'll find her giving her time, talent, and treasures by serving on boards, assisting nonprofits, and connecting people to causes. She is currently working on a creative passion project and turning it into a new business. Stay tuned.

Instagram: cathy.engelman

Brushstrokes of Independence: An Artist's Journey

Sally Evans

"I'll walk where my own nature leads." - Emily Bronte

Art has been part of my life for as long as I can remember. My mother will tell you I started drawing our four Siamese cats when I was just two years old. Later in elementary school, I was taking painting classes at the Boca Raton Art Guild. I was pulled into something that felt less like a choice and more like a calling. I often say I didn't choose art—art chose me. And because I've always loved animals, they became my first subjects.

My childhood was a patchwork of southern towns, stitched together by my father's careers. Each move left a mark, but what remained constant was my love of art. I was born Sally Anne Chastain on May 9,1964. My sister Susan and I were born in Charlotte, NC, where we lived until I was four. Then came Macon, Ga., for two years, and after that, Boca Raton, Fla., for seven. My father, a native Floridian, felt at home in the sunshine and salt air, and my mother (who grew up in South Texas) was just as happy in tropical weather. My sister and I were spoiled living in warm weather, going to the beach, and being outside all year. The tropical landscape and the ocean became a part of me, and Florida suited us all. Eventually, my dad's jobs pulled us to Savannah, Ga., and then Columbia, SC, in 1980.

At Spring Valley High School in Columbia, I found myself surrounded by teachers who recognized my passion and talent. They entered my work in national competitions, and to my surprise, I kept winning awards. I wasn't creating art to collect ribbons; I was creating because it was the thing I loved most. I entered the University of South Carolina in 1982, where I earned a BFA in graphic design with a minor in fine art, as I thought my future might be in marine biology or medical illustration. My brain was not built for math, and three more years of graduate school with cadavers was a *big no*! I've always been very independent, and I was ready to be out of school and on my own.

After graduation, I became a graphic designer. For seven years, I worked in the corporate world—steady, reliable, uninspiring. On weekends, I painted in watercolors, a medium I was devoted to for many years.

I hadn't expected to fall in love with Arizona until my then-husband suggested a trip to Scottsdale in 1991. I resisted because of my love for the ocean and scuba diving. I thought the desert had nothing to offer me and was brown. Once I saw the art, the landscape, and what the artists were creating in unapologetically bold colors, something clicked. I came home and decided I could do this full-time. In 1992, I quit my corporate job and never looked back.

At the same time, I immersed myself in the life and work of Georgia O'Keeffe. She was a maverick in her day and a woman who opened doors for artists like me. For my thirtieth birthday, I made my first trek out to Santa Fe and Ghost Ranch. I spent many years in the 2000s painting the New Mexico landscape, and I feel it's my best and most free work.

What I didn't realize in 1992 was that I would be a small business owner, an entrepreneur, and, in many ways, a warrior. I also realized how lonely the job was. The art world demands resilience, and you need a tough skin to handle the critiques, the uncertainty, the constant reinvention. I worked many part-time jobs to support my painting. Retail work, managing an artist's business and studio, nude modeling for adult art classes, and the most unforgettable one, teaching art in the Department of Corrections in Columbia, SC.

At thirty, I started teaching watercolor painting to inmates convicted of everything from theft to murder. That first night of teaching, I was terrified. During a break, I stepped out with a guard, and when I returned, every supply I'd brought was gone—paints, paper, brushes. They were testing me. I looked at them and said, "If those supplies don't come back, I'm walking out, and I won't return. This is all we have for the entire year." When I stepped back into the room, everything was piled neatly in the center of the table. I had to laugh. It was their way of saying, "We'll push you, but we'll respect you if you stand your ground." That year taught me as much about humanity, resilience, and humor as it did about teaching art.

In the '90s and early 2000s, I sold my paintings through a couple of galleries. I often stayed with my grandmother (a direct descendant of the poet Emily Dickinson's family) in Kerrville, Tex., whose influence shaped my upbringing. At the Hill Country Arts Foundation, mentors like Bill Herring inspired me; after his 1997 workshop, I returned to acrylics and began creating bolder, more colorful work.

That same year, a move to Dunedin, Fla., changed everything for my career. My ex-husband took a job in the Tampa Bay area, and the move opened doors I hadn't even known were waiting.

Syd Entel Galleries in Safety Harbor, Fla., gave me national exposure, and soon my work was published by Winn Devon, then one of the biggest art publishers in the country. My lithographs sold around the world, landing in hotels and various venues, including TV and movies. My paintings have been collected by celebrities, corporations, and even the American Embassy in Rome. I was creating whimsical paintings of my dogs and cats that began winning awards and led to my pet portrait commissions. Meanwhile, my vibrant Florida landscapes, especially my palm tree series, caught the eye of my publisher and festival directors. They became posters and T-shirts for big art festivals across the state and beyond.

I volunteered at the Clearwater Marine Aquarium, where I met the founder of the Outdoor Arts Foundation. Through that connection, I painted on numerous sculptures that raised funds for the aquarium and other charities around Tampa Bay. At the same time, I joined the Junior League of Clearwater-Dunedin, where I learned the importance of supporting women and children. My art also became a way to give back to local Humane

Societies and other animal rescues, causes that have always been close to my heart.

In the early 2000s, *plein air* events were gaining momentum across the country. These were gatherings of artists—painting for days, selling work to support local causes. This was connecting me with a wider community of painters.

In 2008, my marriage ended, and the recession left me broke. At forty-four, I was divorced, renting a condo in Winter Park with my pets, struggling for work, and starting over. That October brought more devastating news: my young cousin died from a drug overdose.

Upon relocating to Orlando, a big positive was the opportunity to reconnect with artist Tom Sadler, whom I had previously met at *plein air* events. He became both my partner and a source of stability during this challenging period of my life.

The summer of 2009 was especially brutal. In June, I was hit by an eighteen-wheeler—the very day the world lost Farrah Fawcett and Michael Jackson. My grandmother passed at age one-hundred-six-and-a-half on Christmas Day, and I had friends battling stage 3 cancer. A shoulder surgery from the accident has left lingering pain in it and my neck to this day. Without Tom, painting, and our circle of artist friends, I don't know how I would have survived.

Slowly, life began to mend. In 2010, Tom and I were married on the beach on Indian Pass, Fla., during the Forgotten Coast Paint Out. Collectors returned, opportunities reopened, and we eventually bought a home in Altamonte Springs. Looking back, I see those years as proof of something I've always known: art isn't just my career, it's my lifeline.

For fifteen years, Tom and I have exhibited in gallery exhibitions together across Florida, New Mexico, Alabama, and Massachusetts. We've joined many *plein air* events, engaging with fellow artists while painting outdoors. Teaching workshops and classes also allows us to share our expertise.

Life brings challenges, but sharing it with another artist has been a blessing. We have shared business opportunities with each other, and we try to balance work life with play. We also remember to pause and live in the moment.

Tom always reminds me, "Don't let the highs get you too high or the lows get you too low." And we like to joke, "We work hard so our cats don't need to."

Now, I'm focused on my artistic legacy and committed to producing my best work. I'm grateful for the gift that has shaped my life and that I can share with others.

This chapter is dedicated to my parents, Linda and David Chastain, who always believed in me and supported my love for art.

About Sally

My paintings are expressive works of contemporary art that are constantly evolving. I paint with a combination of vivid colors, line, and design that constantly challenges me by the emotions I feel when painting. Color has been the focus of my paintings for many years, and my subject matters are inspired by nature and the sense of humor that life has to offer. I want to convey to my viewers that commonplace subjects can be viewed in uncommon ways.

My artworks have been featured in exhibitions and galleries across prominent cities, including New York City, New York; Martha's Vineyard, Mass.; Charleston, SC; Winter Park, Fla.; and Taos, NM, to name a few.

Currently, my paintings are showcased at the US Airways Club in Tampa International Airport. Notably, my work was also displayed in the American Embassy in Rome through the Art and Embassies Program in 2001. Over the years, my pieces have been selected as featured art for numerous festivals in Florida and the covers of magazines including *Tampa Bay Magazine* and *The New Barker*. Locally, my piece "Lilies Dance in Light" served as the signature artwork for the Winter Autumn Art Festival in 2013. Over the years, my lithographs have been featured on the television series *Nip/Tuck* and the films *American Dreamz* and *Shock and Awe*.

My work is included in various corporate collections, such as *Tampa Bay Magazine*, the US Airways Club at Tampa International Airport, The St. Joe Company, Coca-Cola Corporation, Chili's Corporation, Walker and Company Inc. (Winter Park, Fla.), and Christie Lites (Orlando, Fla.).

www.sallyevans.com
Instagram: sallyevansfineart
Facebook: Contemporary Art and Pet Portraits by Sally Evans
YouTube: Sally Evans Fine Art

A Life Designed with Grace

DeDe DeWine Holloway

I grew up a Texas girl with an amazing family. My parents raised my brother Tom and me in the Catholic church, giving us both a foundation of faith and a personal relationship with Jesus. Weekends were filled with tennis matches, family outings, and simple joys that grounded me in values I carry to this day. I am especially grateful to my parents, Dennis and Cheryl. My dad was an entrepreneur and business owner of multiple real estate offices throughout Texas, and his advice has guided me many times in life and business. My mom taught me the art and business of making a home—first for my family, then for myself, and ultimately for the clients I now serve.

After graduating from design school in Dallas, life took me on a journey I could never have imagined. In the early '90s, I married an Englishman and moved to North London. The shift from sunny Texas to the gray, damp weather of England was only the beginning of the adjustments I had to make. I quickly learned to adapt to a wide range of accents, cultural traditions, and the daily routines of life as a wife and eventually a mother in England.

My husband's family welcomed me with open arms, and I grew especially close with his mum, Pearl, and his sister, Kim. Those relationships and dear friends I made, became anchors as I settled into my new life. London became the backdrop of some of my most cherished years. Taylor and Morgan were born there, and I became "Mummy," a name they still call me to this day.

Pearl and I spent countless hours shopping together, wandering through the shops of London, and taking in the city's architecture and history. We attended home shows to explore the latest trends, and I found myself fascinated by the blend of tradition and innovation that shaped English design. Meanwhile, my young girls kept me busy with play groups, ballet practice, cooking, and baking. I embraced being a stay-at-home mum, and those years reminded me of my own mother, who had always made our home such a place of comfort and warmth. The memories of that season remain precious to me, and they planted the seeds of my love for interiors that would later grow into a career.

After seven years in the UK, our family moved to Orlando, Fla., in September of 1999. Ten years later, life shifted dramatically when I found myself a divorced, single mother with a new home, bills to pay, and two daughters looking to me for stability. What had once been a hobby needed to become a career. In 2010, DeWine Design was born.

In the very beginning, my business did not look like the full-service design studio it is today. I actually started as a mural artist, painting walls all over Orlando. From college and professional sports logos to faux finishes, from residential spaces to restaurants and doctors' offices, I poured my creativity into every project. Believe it or not, some of those murals are still standing today. Not long ago, a friend sent me a photo of one of my murals in a pediatric doctor's office, taken while she was there with her grandson. It reminded me of those humble beginnings and how each brushstroke in those years was building the foundation of the career I have now.

At first, it was word of mouth and small kitchen projects. I posted photos on Facebook, and kind clients left heartfelt reviews. Slowly, my little business gained traction. In 2012, I began dating my college boyfriend, Sacha, who believed in me and encouraged me to grow my brand. Together with trusted renovation contractors, I started building a business with a waitlist. During that time, Sacha was battling stage four melanoma. Despite his fight, he never stopped encouraging me. His strength showed me what true resilience looks like. When he passed away in 2015, I was devastated. Yet in the middle of grief, his words kept echoing in my heart. He had always reminded me to see the big picture, and I knew I had to keep going, both for my daughters and for myself.

The months that followed were heavy. I leaned on my family, friends, and faith. My clients were patient, giving me space to grieve and rebuild. I reminded myself of what it means to be Texas Tough. With a mortgage, a daughter in college, and another in high school, I knew I had no choice but to persevere.

Almost a year after Sacha's passing, a friend convinced me to go out to dinner. That evening led me to eventually meet a man named Gary on a blind date, set up by a mutual friend. I wasn't ready for a relationship, but as we talked, I discovered that we shared more than a spark. Gary was also in the renovation field, and our conversations naturally gravitated toward projects, ideas, and visions. We soon took a leap of faith together, investing in a large teardown property. I handled the design and finishes while Gary led the build team. By the time the house sold a year later, we had not only completed a successful flip but also discovered a partnership that extended into love and life.

Gary quickly became my best friend, my partner in every sense of the word, and the person who reminded me how to laugh again. He never asked me to erase the memories of Sacha. Instead, he embraced my story, my daughters, and my family. With him, I felt whole again. We leaned into the growing popularity of HGTV's design shows, highlighting our unique husband-and-wife dynamic. DeWine Design thrived, thanks not only to my design work, but also to Gary's cabinet expertise and house-flipping skills. Together, with our amazing contractors, we became a team that clients could trust completely.

In February 2020, Gary and I were married at Casa Feliz in Winter Park, Fla. It was a magical day surrounded by our closest family and friends—a dream come true. When we returned from our honeymoon in Jamaica, the world shut down with the arrival of the pandemic. Both of my daughters moved back home, and while the world outside was uncertain, I felt incredibly blessed. That unexpected season gave me cherished time with them under one roof again, a gift I would not have had if not for the pause the pandemic created.

By 2021, I knew it was time to get back to business. We had a waitlist of clients eager to move forward once restrictions lifted. Living in Florida, Gary and I were considered essential as licensed contractors, which allowed us to carefully step back into work. In that season, I made one of the most pivotal decisions of my career.

I invested in an interior design business coach. At the time, the investment felt enormous and the timing uncertain, but I knew it was not just about my company. It was an investment in myself.

Michelle's year-long program gave me what I had been missing—systems, processes, and structure. I dedicated myself to the training, often waking at five in the morning to study the modules. It paid off almost immediately. One of my new projects covered the cost of the program three times over. More than that, the coaching community opened my eyes to something I hadn't expected. I discovered that I truly loved mentoring others. After I graduated, Michelle invited me to serve as a master coach for my experience in kitchen and bathroom design. It was an honor, and it reignited a new layer of passion within me.

Stepping into the role of mentor has been one of the most fulfilling surprises of my career. I love watching other designers succeed, knowing that something I shared gave them the clarity or confidence to move forward. It brings me so much joy to see their businesses grow, their confidence increase, and their visions come to life. Offering advice that adds real value, not only to their projects but to the coaching program as a whole, has been deeply rewarding. The same program that transformed my own business gave me the opportunity to give back, and in doing so, I discovered a new layer of purpose. Being part of someone else's success story is a gift, and it continues to inspire me to pour into others just as I was poured into.

As DeWine Design grew, I built a small team of designers and moved into a dedicated studio space. We rebranded with a new logo and website, presenting ourselves as a boutique full-service interior design firm. The projects expanded in scope and visibility, and in September 2025, DeWine Design Interiors received its first design award for a recent bathroom project. That recognition felt like a milestone, a tangible reflection of years of perseverance, faith, and growth.

Through it all, I have been lifted by my husband, my daughters, my family, and my friends. Their support carried me through times when I doubted my strength. Yet I am also proud of myself for holding fast to my faith, for refusing to quit, and for proving to my daughters what it looks like to rise after loss.

When I received the message from Leigh inviting me to contribute to *Slaying Orlando*, I felt a rush of gratitude. To be included among women who have lived boldly and endured hardship but still chose to thrive is an honor I do not take lightly. My story is one of family, faith, perseverance, and love. It is about loss and renewal, heartbreak and joy, failure and triumph. It is proof that you can start again, rebuild, and create something beautiful—not just in business, but in life.

As I look back, I see how every chapter prepared me for the next. The lessons from my parents, the years in England, the challenges of single motherhood, the love and loss of Sacha, and the new beginning with Gary have all shaped me. Each trial refined my strength, and each blessing reminded me of the power of faith and resilience. Being part of *Slaying Orlando* is not only about sharing my journey, but also about standing alongside incredible women who prove every day that no matter what life throws at us, we can rise, we can thrive, and we can slay.

About DeDe

DeDe DeWine Holloway is the founder and principal designer of DeWine Design Interiors, a boutique luxury interior design firm based in Orlando, Fla. With a design degree from the Art Institute of Dallas and years of experience living abroad in London, she brings a global perspective to her work, blending refined creativity with approachable warmth. She is deeply grateful to her parents, Dennis and Cheryl, who instilled the foundation of her success. Her father, an entrepreneur and owner of multiple real estate offices across Texas, shared invaluable business advice and guidance. Her mother taught her the art and business of making a home, lessons that shaped not only her own family life but also the way she designs beautiful, functional spaces for her clients.

In 2010, DeDe launched DeWine Design Interiors, transforming what began as a personal passion into an award-winning business. Her firm specializes in luxury residential renovations, turnkey remodels, and curated furnishings, creating spaces that feel both elevated and effortless. Under her leadership, DeWine Design Interiors has grown into a full-service studio with a trusted team, recognized in 2025 with its first design award.

Beyond client projects, DeDe is deeply involved in her community. She is an active member of Rotary International, where she has served for more than ten years. She is also an active member of the Interior Design Society and serves as a coach for fellow designers, drawing on her expertise in kitchens, bathrooms, and business strategy to mentor others.

When she is not designing, DeDe enjoys traveling, playing tennis, and spending time with her husband Gary, her daughters, her family, and her dear friends.

https://dewinedesign.com/
Instagram: www.instagram.com/dewinedesign/
Facebook: www.facebook.com/dewinedesign
Houzz: https://www.houzz.com/pro/dede-aspery/__public
Linkedin: https://www.linkedin.com/in/dededewineholloway/

The Basement of the Kremlin

Rinat Halon Neal

It is just after seven a.m. in Moscow, Russia, and the sky is gray and gloomy as the driver of our van pulls up to one of the Kremlin gates and stops. A Russian guard carrying a rifle with his finger hovering over the trigger approaches.

I am in the back, with bags of rented studio photography equipment at my feet. My driver rolls down his window and hands the Kremlin guard our papers. It is so quiet, I can hear myself breathe.

The guard inspects our papers, looks up at me, and back at the documents. No muscle moves on his stoic face. How would he feel if he knew I was an Israeli American Jew? He does not know. Would he care? I am alone in a foreign, generally unfriendly country, willingly entering the Kremlin's basement for a magazine photoshoot.

It sounded like a great idea a week ago, when the phone rang and Dolores Kondrashova, head coach of the Russian hairdressing team, had a question for me. Imagine the winner of the hairdressing world championship, Hairworld in Seoul (the first time Russia won the World Champion title) and the founder of the Academy of Hairstyling in Moscow, Russia, asking if I would photograph the models for her upcoming Wella Master Hairdresser styling show.

"Oh, and it will be at the Kremlin," added Dolores's translator while Dolores kept speaking in Russian in the background.

Of course it will be at the Kremlin. "Go big or go home" was the only way for Dolores.

I loved that woman from the moment I met her when she was in her seventies, this beautiful businesswoman, a powerhouse, sitting behind her enormous black wooden desk, full makeup on, and her blond hair layered perfectly over her forehead. Who would know she had partial paralysis and speech impairment from a stroke a few years earlier? I approached as Dolores yelled commands in Russian to her staff. I sensed her authoritative presence as I watched her staff run around to fulfill her instructions.

The guard waves my driver on as he opens the Kremlin gates. "*Spasiba*," (thank you), says my driver, and we drive in silence until we soon reach the Kremlin building and park. My driver gets out, and the gravel crunches under his feet. He slides open the van's side door, which creaks in protest.

I step out, and as I reach in for my camera bag, I see three Kremlin guards approaching. I put on a brave front as my heart sinks. Without a word, the first Kremlin guard reaches over. I panic, thinking he will grab me. Then, he and the other two guards reach behind me for my photo equipment bags. I breathe in deeply, and hope they cannot hear my loudly beating heart.

Okay. Now what?

Dolores loved me from the moment we met. Whenever I flew to Russia with her nephew, my then fiancé, I would walk into her home or office, and she would smile with joy. Which always turned into a big sigh as she ranted in Russian, waving her hands, rattled about my hair—big, uncontrolled, bouncing curls. She wanted to blow them dry straight into a neat, elegant hairstyle. She never did it, though. She accepted me as I was.

The first Kremlin guard—who I guess is an officer—walks toward the door with my studio light bag, then turns around and waves me over. I straighten my camera gear bag on my back and walk over to stand behind him. Then, the other two guards, each with a photography equipment bag, form a line behind me. The officer opens the door, and off we march ahead, me and the guards, into the Kremlin building.

The officer leads us through dim, tight corridors with scant headroom. I focus on the officer. *Right, left, right, left, right, left,* I play the steps from my Israeli Defense Forces basic training as I march with the Russian soldiers in a synchronized rhythm.

Dolores came to Russia as a young Armenian immigrant in the 1970s. She was poor and worked hard for many years as a hairdresser to survive before her luck changed through a chance meeting with an oligarch who loved her style and told everyone about her. The rest is history. One evening, while visiting her beautiful Moscow home, Dolores stood in the kitchen, wearing her robe and hair net, by the stunning gold faucets. She described the moment she knew everything had changed. Simon, my ex-fiancé, translated from Russian to Hebrew. "I was closing the hair salon for the night, and I placed the money we made that day in the salon's safe. We had made so much money, the safe would not close!" Dolores made grand gestures, mimicking her efforts to close the safe overflowing with rubles.

Dolores was the first self-made female millionaire I had met. I immediately recognized a once-in-a-lifetime opportunity to learn from the great. No language, culture, or age differences would stop me from connecting with this amazing woman I admired so much.

We walk down a long staircase; I smell mold and hold onto the walls for safety, hoping I do not touch it. Suddenly, the officer opens a door in the dim corridor, and we walk into a big, well-lit area. Without a word, the Russian guards drop off my equipment bags and disappear. I stand alone in a spacious area large enough to set up a studio. I pull out my backdrop stands and set up the background. I set up the main, fill, and key lights, check my camera settings, and make sure the lights fire. Now, I am ready for the photoshoot.

On the phone a week ago, Dolores said in Russian, "You will photograph the models before they go on stage." I answered in English, "Thank you, Dolores, for giving me this opportunity. I know you can get any photographer you want to do this job, and I appreciate the chance." I heard the translator repeat my grateful words in Russian, and Dolores answered through him, "You deserve it. You are talented and determined. I know you can make it big. Enjoy this photoshoot!"

While I wait, I decide to check out the area. The intense smell of hairspray leads me down a lit hallway, where rooms are bustling with show preparation activity: Hairdressers buzz around in a flurry of hair clips, brushes, and curling irons, creating hair designs like I have never seen before! The models have structured towers of hair shaped into remarkable designs that would shame some architectural fixtures. Camouflaged by the loud hair dryers, I stay out of sight and snap some black-and-white shots of the getting-ready scenes unfolding in front of me. I walk back to my studio set up and wait.

Then, the first model appears from the prep rooms, hardly able to walk straight with that construction on her head. She steps onto my white backdrop. I had learned a few photoshoot-related words in Russian. I pick up my camera and say:

"*Glaza zdies*" (eyes here). The model, trying to stay balanced, looks at me, and I click the shutter.

"*Podborodok vverkh*" (chin up). The model looks the other way with her chin up; I click the shutter.

Then, she walks off my backdrop.

At that moment, I realize this IS the photoshoot—the only time before the models go up on stage. As the next model walks onto my backdrop, my mind goes into intense focus. I feel myself rising to this new level of professionalism and work in quiet calm. In Russian, I give each model direction, snap a few shots, until soon, they are all gone, walking to the Kremlin stage for the hair show. The photoshoot is over.

Everything I ever learned in my then twelve-year professional photography career came together in those few precious moments, allowing me to create magazine-worthy images. What if I didn't know how to calculate light ratios, how to pose, how to give directions in the model's language, or what equipment to rent for this shoot?

What if I didn't trust Dolores and wouldn't walk into the Kremlin by myself?

In so many ways, this photoshoot could have turned disastrous.

But it didn't.

The following month, the new issue of the *Dolores Magazine* drops hot off the press and lands on my desk. I pause before working up the courage to open it. I flip through the pages, and stop when I arrive at the first page of the article about the Walla Hair Show in the Kremlin. My heart skips a beat. Dolores added the black-and-white shots of the models getting ready to the magazine layout. I tear up with gratitude and flip to the next page to see a photo of the model staring at me, filling the entire page, taken in my makeshift studio in the Kremlin basement. Opposite, another model photo I created, full page! I flip the page again, coming head-on with two more of my pictures of the beautiful models. Flipping the page—two more pages with my photographs.

On the final page of the story, I see the production credits. All in Russian, except my name. My photography credit is in English. Dolores knew I was not seeking a photography career in Russia and that I wanted to move back to the United States, so she ensured the photography credit was in English, allowing anyone in the Western world to know I took these shots.

God, I loved that woman!

I did a few more photography assignments for Dolores before I left Russia for good. The last time Dolores and I spoke was two years after the Kremlin shoot when I was living in Tel Aviv, Israel. My phone rang. To my surprise, Dolores's translator said, "Dolores wants to speak with you." Nervous and excited, I said, "Of course!" Her familiar voice filled my heart with joy. I could hear the effort in her post-stroke voice when Dolores, determined as always, said to me slowly, in English:

"I love you."

I answered, in Russian:

"*Ya lublook te-bea.*"

I love you, too.

That *Dolores Magazine* feature I photographed over sixteen years ago is still on display in my Florida studio. I love showing it to clients; the model's hairstyle designs blow them away. Dolores was a visionary. A strong businesswoman with an incredibly kind heart and a creative spark that lit the world of hair design on fire.

I will always treasure the chance Dolores gave me to rise to the next level of my craft and be amazing.

Even though it was scary, tough, and challenging, I proved to myself that I can do it. Which engraved inspiration into my soul, ready for me to use every time a growth opportunity presents itself now and forever. Thank you, Dolores!

About Rinat

Rinat Halon Neal is an internationally published, award-winning photographer whose twenty-eight-year career spans the globe. An Israeli-American dual citizen raised in Tel Aviv and Columbus, Ohio, her professional journey began at sixteen as a child actress-singer on Israeli television. At eighteen, she served two years in the Israeli military, entertaining with the USO branch. She later earned a personalized honors degree in photography and visual merchandising from The Ohio State University, writing a thesis on photography's influence on purchasing behavior.

Across her career, Rinat has photographed high-ranking government officials, celebrities, weddings, culinary arts, high fashion, jewelry, architecture, and more. Her work has appeared in magazines and exhibitions internationally; five of her photographs are part of the permanent collection of the Israeli congress. She earned a "Superior Artist" award in Israel and Distinguished Honor in the Florida Professional Photographers Print Competition.

Today, Rinat serves clients throughout Central Florida and travels internationally for commissioned work, creating heirloom portraits and brand imagery that blend technical mastery with authentic storytelling. She holds the PPA craftsman degree and is a certified professional photographer; she has served on the Professional Photographers of America Council, and she has taught at Rollins College's Center for Lifelong Learning, as well as photography guilds worldwide. Rinat is also the author of the instructional book, *What's Wrong with My Camera?* Her guiding mission is simple: to help every person see that they are, in fact, photogenic—so their beauty, story, and legacy can live on in portraits for generations to come.

https://www.rinathalon.com/
Facebook: https://www.facebook.com/rinat.halon/
Instagram: https://www.instagram.com/rinathalon/
LinkedIn: https://www.linkedin.com/in/rinathalon/

Legacy of Grace, Threads of Strength

Endsley Hewitt

I was born exactly one day past my due date, making my entrance into the world as destiny would have it on my Dad's thirty-sixth birthday, just as my mom had predicted. I entered *en caul*, wrapped in my amniotic sac. A rare birth, the doctor told my parents, I was a "special one." From my very first breath, my story was tied to legacy, to family, and to a sense of being set apart.

I grew up in St. Petersburg, Fla., a city wrapped in sunshine and salt air. My childhood was marked by sandy feet, boat rides, and fishing trips, but the heart of every summer was Little Gasparilla Island. I can still see myself on the dock, watching for the seaweed to peek through the water, a sure sign the tide was low and it was time to go clamming. My sister and I would wade through the bay in our old Keds, waiting to feel the smooth bulge of a clam hiding beneath the sand. I never cared much for eating them, but I loved the ritual, digging with my mom, dad, and sister, filling the bucket, laughing until the sun slipped low.

By the end of every summer, my blonde hair had turned nearly white from the sun, my skin was tan, and my heart was full. Swinging in the hammock on the porch, I was simply a happy girl soaking up a season that felt endless. Those salt-soaked days have stayed with me long after. My name, Endsley, carries the weight of legacy. It was my Grandma Vera's maiden name, and I've always felt tethered to the quiet strength and grace of the woman who came before me.

Even as those summers shaped me, another part of me was dreaming bigger than the bay. Between hammock swings and glossy magazines, I imagined a world where I could step into the beauty and confidence I saw on those pages. By my teenage years, that dream began to take shape. Modeling entered my life. At first thrilling and terrifying, it soon became more than an opportunity. It became a calling, one that carried me beyond St. Pete into lessons I could have never learned barefoot on the dock.

My parents, strong believers in education, weren't against me modeling but made it clear that if I pursued it, it would be on my own. At nineteen, I left for the University of Florida (UF) with a dream of writing for a fashion magazine and earning my degree in journalism.

Within three weeks, life surprised me in the most extraordinary way. I was set up on a blind date with a boy named Thomas, the man who would change everything. I'll never forget racing home to my apartment that night and leaving a message on my parents' answering machine that began, "I just met the man I'm going to marry."

Two years at UF flew by. Thomas, two years older, had graduated and returned to Orlando to work in commercial real estate with his family. I couldn't imagine being separated from him. I accelerated my studies, graduated a year early, and moved to Orlando for love. We were engaged soon after and married just shy of my twenty-second birthday.

Once in Orlando, I submitted photos to agencies and quickly found myself modeling nonstop.

The early 2000s were booming in Florida fashion. I shot weekly for Beall's and Dillard's and often drove across the state for runway shows with Neiman Marcus and Saks. It was an exciting time. I had the chance to model for and meet designers like Carmen Marc, Volvo, Mark Badgley, and James Mischka, each experience another surreal reminder that the girl from St. Pete with sandy feet had stepped into the glossy pages she once dreamed of.

Two and a half years later, our first son, Watson, arrived. I modeled until six months along, then returned to work when he was just six weeks old. At twenty-five, balancing life as a model, wife, and new mother was demanding, but I had always dreamed of motherhood, and from the moment they placed his nine-pound, eleven-ounce body in my arms, I knew this role would forever be my highest calling.

Three years later, our second son, Pierson, arrived through a traumatic cesarean delivery, and in that moment, we knew our family was complete. Motherhood became my center. From the beginning, Thomas and I promised to raise our boys with intention, prioritizing the quality of their childhood over the quantity of our schedules. That promise became the heartbeat of our home.

Those early years were filled with the small defining adventures of childhood, each one a reminder of the promises we'd made. Watson, our green-thumbed "green tween," started a garden club and turned his fresh herbs into a little soap business called Watsoap. Soon, music captured his heart, and he fell in love with the towering double bass, a creative outlet that grounded him through high school. Saturdays belonged to football, with Thomas coaching both boys from the sidelines, turning the field into another kind of classroom. Pierson, our gifted fisherman, begged to fish every spare weekend we had at our family's island house on little Gasparilla, casting from dusk to dawn. Eventually, he launched his own fishing rod company, Captiva Customs, out of a passion for rod building he shared with my dad.

Legacy runs deep in our family. It isn't something we take lightly, but a value we talk about often. The threads of faith, love, and shared passion connect us across generations, and it's a tradition I hope both of my boys will carry forward.

One summer while visiting family in Stuart, I sat at my aunt's kitchen table with my mom, sister, and cousins, swapping family health stories while my boys played. My cousin, a urologist, turned to my mom, his Aunt Diane, and asked if she had ever been tested for the BRCA1 gene mutation, the one linked to a lifetime breast cancer risk of up to eighty-nine percent.

My mom, a two-time breast cancer survivor, said no. Years earlier, she'd been warned that a positive result could cost her health insurance, but the laws had since changed. With his gentle push, she agreed to be tested. Weeks later, the call came: she was BRCA1 positive.

Suddenly the question wasn't just about my mother; it was about my sister and me. Each of us now faced a fifty percent chance of carrying the same mutation. As I peeked out the window, watching my boys play outside, the weight of that possibility felt sharper and far more personal.

I'll never forget the day I found out. I was thirty-three, driving home from a casting in Tampa on a sweltering June afternoon, when my breast specialist called with the results. Positive. As a model, my body had become a part of my identity, photographed, critiqued, celebrated. Now I was being asked to give up the very thing that defined me. Beneath the medical statistics was a haunting fear. Would I still be able to continue working and doing what I loved?

With my boys just seven and four at the time, the choice was clear: I didn't want to live in fear of the day these "little ticking time bombs," as my specialist described them, would implode. Days later, I scheduled a preventative double mastectomy. On September eleventh, I went into a four-hour surgery carrying more than a fear of cancer; I carried the fear of trading in my femininity, the only body I had ever known, to ensure my boys would have a healthy mother.

Recovery was tough. I was a candidate for a nipple-sparing mastectomy, so while I would not have feeling in my breasts, I would still have some familiarity, a blessing I know many women don't have. For the first week, I avoided the mirror. I didn't want negative thoughts to hinder my healing. My mom, who had been with us to help with the boys, encouraged me to look when I returned for my one-week post op appointment to have my drains removed. When I finally did, I braced myself for devastation, but instead I felt something unexpected. Gratitude. My scars didn't take away my beauty; they redefined it. They told the story of a woman who chose life, strength, and faith over fear. I wasn't just a model anymore. I was a survivor, alive for my boys.

At thirty-nine, six years later, I faced another twist. News broke that the textured implants used for my reconstruction were being recalled because they were causing breast cancer; thousands of other women had had these implants. That September, I went back for two more surgeries just weeks apart, a salpingectomy (removing my fallopian tubes to reduce ovarian cancer risk) and the replacement of my textured implants with smooth ones. Both procedures were far easier than the first. My boys were fifteen and twelve then, an age I assumed came with understanding, though their memories now remind me how protected they really were.

They say knowledge is power, and for me, learning that I was BRCA1 positive became exactly that: the power to choose to live. Through every surgery, every scar, every step of recovery, my faith anchored me. My mantra came from Numbers 6:24, "The Lord bless you and keep you, the Lord make His face shine upon you and be gracious to you, the Lord turn his face toward you and give you peace." I chose this verse before my first surgery, and when I walked into the hospital for my pre-op appointment, I saw it hanging in huge letters on the wall. I knew God was reminding me He was with me then and always.

Life marched on with all the chaos of raising two boys, until the day my soul was shaken in a way it never had been before. We said goodbye to my dad, my Gemini birthday twin, Pop Pop to my boys, an attorney, a fisherman, and a man who gave his heart to Jesus. He served at his church weekly, leading by quiet, steady example. Losing him cracked my heart wide open.

Grief has a way of changing you. It doesn't leave, it reshapes. It made me more empathetic, more tender, and more intentional about how I lived each day. It taught me that nothing is promised and everything we love is fragile.

Today, I stand in a season of gratitude and reinvention. My younger son will head to college next fall, signaling the close of one chapter of family life and the beginning of another. I've been blessed to continue modeling into my forties—and each new season I spend surrounded by my modeling family reminds me what a gift this career has been.

At the same time, my heart has been pulled back to writing and storytelling. From my own journey to the children's books inspired by our Labradoodle, Fiona. Life keeps teaching me that beauty lives far beneath the surface. It's in the soul, in showing up, in loving deeply, and trusting God with every step.

I move forward, certain that each day will be filled with grace, purpose, and possibility.

About Endsley

Endsley Hewitt is a professional fashion model, writer, and creative entrepreneur with more than twenty-five years of experience in front of the camera. Throughout her career, she has modeled for iconic brands including Saks Fifth Avenue, Neiman Marcus, Dillard's, and Nordstrom. She balances the glamour of fashion with a grounded devotion to family and community.

As a wife and mother of two sons, Endsley has always embraced the many chapters of womanhood with grace and authenticity. She recently entered a new season of reinvention, blending her modeling career with her passion for writing, design, and storytelling. She is currently developing *Fancy Fiona*, a whimsical children's book series inspired by her beloved Labradoodle. It weaves gentle life lessons with sparkle, heart, and imagination.

Outside of her creative work, Endsley is deeply engaged in her community. She was previously on the board for the Young Men's Service League, and also served as assistant VP of membership and VP of communications. She continues to volunteer there with her son while supporting families and organizations across Central Florida. She also shares her love of fashion, interior design, and wellness through lifestyle content. It inspires others to embrace beauty not just in how life looks, but in how deeply it is lived.

Endsley believes in the power of reinvention, the strength of family, and the joy of pursuing creative dreams. Her story is a reminder that beauty evolves with each chapter and that purpose and passion are timeless.

@endsleyhewitt on all social media

The Escape Artist

Ansley Highland

I used to call myself "The Escape Artist." I had a twenty-year career in jewelry and garden design, a passion for fashion and style, and a love of writing music and poetry like my grandmother. Creativity always sparkled on the surface. But underneath? It was buried beneath fear, shame, and survival.

I wasn't creating my life. I was using creativity to escape the one I was living.

What I didn't realize was that my True Self had been there all along, yearning to use her true voice. She had been adjusting, performing, suppressing so she could belong and be loved. But she never stopped whispering reminders of her power, purpose, originality, and joy.

My remembering began when everything I had built collapsed at once: my marriage, my forty-year religious foundation, and more than half of my closest relationships. It was chaos, confusion, heartbreak. A true crash and burn. But in the rubble, I had an epiphany: *I kept choosing my confusion because I wasn't ready to choose my power.*

At some point, I realized that if I had created my co-dependent chaos, maybe I could create something else: empowered clarity and conscious creativity! The shift was subtle, but powerful: *I no longer had to create to escape my life; I could instead create a life I didn't want to escape.*

This realization became my soul's assignment: to throw off fear—which had been sitting like a wet blanket over my creative gifts—and align my personal creative power with my soul's purpose. To become an energy alchemist, transforming anxiety into creativity. Not once, but as a way of life.

It was there all along. My True Self's creative spark, asking to light up my life and then light up the world.

Conscious Creativity: Waking Up to Presence

When everything fell apart, anxiety became my constant companion. It wasn't subtle anymore— it was loud, insistent, and exhausting. At first, I fought it, trying to silence the symptoms through busyness and denial. But eventually, I realized anxiety wasn't my enemy. It was my invitation.

Anxiety was the alarm bell telling me I was out of alignment with my True Self. It was survival energy running the show. And if energy can't be destroyed, only transformed, then what if I could learn to transform that anxious energy into creative energy?

That's when I began practicing *presence*. This awareness of my breath, body, and beliefs became my anchor. It taught me that creativity doesn't begin in the mind; it begins in the Holy Now. When I could pause, breathe, and notice—not numbing, not running, but actually being—I began to create from an entirely different place.

In presence, I could see that I wasn't broken. I didn't need to prove, perform, or perfect to belong. I could simply *be*. And in that being, I tapped into a deep consciousness that was always available: the certainty of possibility.

Anxiety used to spiral me into the future or trap me in the past. But presence gave me a way to alchemize it, turning *racing thoughts into rhythm* and *panic into possibility*. I realized I wasn't just surviving my life anymore. I was beginning to consciously create it.

Connection: Belonging to Myself Again

As presence steadied me, I realized something even deeper: I had spent my whole life trying to belong everywhere...except to myself.

I knew how to adapt, adjust, and abandon pieces of who I was to gain acceptance. But true connection didn't begin outside of me. It began when I stopped betraying my True Self for approval and started listening to her voice again.

She spoke through my intuition, through sparks of creativity, through the tug in my soul that longed for truth and freedom. Learning to tune into that voice was like finding an inner compass and true spiritual connection I didn't know I had. I had been taught to distrust her and outsource my inner authority to systems—religion, family, culture, career. Self-abandonment was dressed up as selflessness! But I was learning how to reclaim my belonging. Sometimes the shift was quiet and subtle; other times, it surged through me like lightning, but it always led me toward more alignment, more authenticity, and more love.

Connection also meant I could let joy belong as much as sorrow, let my intuition belong as much as logic, let my True Self belong as much as the roles I had once played to survive.

And here's the paradox: when I began belonging to myself, I found I could belong anywhere. I no longer needed external validation to prove I was worthy of love. The joy in my soul started rising to the surface again, not forced or performed, but true.

From this place of joy and connection, my creativity shifted, too. The more I trusted my own voice, the freer my creative voice became. It was no longer about impressing, but about *expressing* my soul. Creativity was no longer about seeking attention, but offering connection and transformation.

Co-creation: Creating Beauty with and for Others

From the soil of presence and the roots of connection, creativity began to bloom again—only this time not as escape, but as expression. And not just for me, but with and for others.

Dora Mae Jewelry became one of the first places I lived this reality. Clients bring me heirloom diamonds, forgotten brooches, tangled chains, pieces that have been sitting in drawers for ages because their owners might see them as too outdated, too broken, too "not me." My favorite part isn't just the transformation of the jewelry itself, but the transformation I see in the woman holding it. Together, we dream. We play. We peel back layers until her style, her story, her True Self shines again in a piece she'll actually wear.

So the piece becomes so much more than a jewel: it becomes a symbol. A reminder that beauty was never lost, but waiting to be reimagined.

But my creativity couldn't be contained in gemstones alone. The same current that ran through my jewelry design started running through my pen. I began writing about the very shifts I was living–presence, connection, alignment, embodiment, completion. What started as personal notes to keep myself afloat became frameworks for my upcoming book, *Creativity in Bloom*, and my *True Self Challenge*. These weren't abstract ideas. They were lived maps, breadcrumbs left behind for anyone else trying to find their way out of self-abandonment and into freedom.

To me, co-creation means my healing serves your healing. My freedom gives permission for your freedom. My *you*-ness strengthens our *one*-ness. When I align my creative power with my soul's purpose, it multiplies—expanding not just my life, but the lives it touches.

I no longer create to escape my life; I create to expand it. I create to remind others that when everything in life seems to die, we have the choice to merely *survive in the rubble* OR to create something new...and LIVE. I watched it all crash and burn. I chose to rise from the ashes. And I'm still rising.

If there's one thing my journey has taught me, it's this: you are not broken, and you are not behind. You *already are*. Beneath the layers of fear, shame, and survival, your True Self is alive and waiting to create through you.

The same power I use to reimagine heirlooms, to rewrite my story, to rise from the ashes—that same creative spark is in you. You don't have to wait until you're more ready, more perfect, more certain.

You just have to begin...to breathe, to be Here, to belong to yourself. And then create—not to escape, not to impress, but to connect, expand, and transform. Create the life you don't want to escape. Create from your joy, from your pain, from your love.

And as you do, you'll remember: your *you*-ness really does serve our *one*-ness. And when you use your unique and soulful creative gifts, it really IS the greatest love letter you can give to the world!

Creatively Yours,

Ansley

About Ansley

Ansley Highland is a designer, writer, and creative visionary whose work bridges beauty, transformation, and soul. For over twenty years, she has channeled her artistic expression through Dora Mae Jewelry, where heirloom diamonds, forgotten brooches, and vintage treasures are reimagined into modern "everyday heirlooms." But Ansley's soul's purpose extends beyond jewelry to expand both individual and collective creative power—the antidote to a world increasingly shaped by AI, avatars, and algorithms.

Through her writing and teaching, Ansley invites others to reclaim their innate creativity not as performance for attention and validation, but as a path of powerful connection and transformation. She is the founder of *On Being Creative* and the author of *Creativity in Bloom*, a framework that helps people align their unique creative power with their soul's purpose. Her *True Self Challenge* and workshops on creative flow empower participants to unlearn self-abandonment, embrace presence, and embody love and freedom rather than fear and control.

Ansley's own journey of rising from anxiety, perfectionism, and the collapse of her marriage and faith informs every word she writes and every jewel she designs. She believes that creativity is not just what we make—it is how we live. Her mission is to help others stop creating to escape their lives and start creating lives they don't want to escape.

Ansley lives in Orlando, Fla., where she is endlessly inspired by her grandmother's legacy, her children, and the joy of watching creativity spark new life—in jewelry and in gardens, in stories and in souls.

Social media: @doramaejewelry @on.being.creative
www.doramaejewelry.com

From Wounds to Breath, From Silence to Light

Lizbeth Jimenez

I was four when my life split into before and after. My father died suddenly of a heart attack, leaving behind more than grief—he left behind the memory of his fists, the echo of my mother's cries, and a house that had learned to flinch. But the story didn't end clean. When my mother finally found the courage to leave him, his heart gave out soon after. Instead of being held in her liberation, she was blamed. Her own family turned their backs, whispering that she had killed him with her leaving. Shame became our inheritance.

We didn't grow up with money. We grew up with wounds. I remember my mother at the kitchen table, bills spread like a puzzle she couldn't solve, the radio playing soft to drown out worry. I watched her believe that stability had to arrive on the arm of a man, and I watched her cycle through relationships that bruised her spirit all over again. Those choices left footprints that I would follow for years.

When I was six, maybe seven, people who should have protected me became the ones who hurt me most. Family members touched me in ways that carved shame into my bones. When I finally spoke that truth, the response was cruel and swift: I was too provocative, they said. I had asked for it. Imagine being a little girl and learning that your pain is somehow your fault. That shame sank deep and made a home inside me, bending the way I moved through the world.

School became another battlefield. I was jumped, bullied, targeted by girls who saw me as competition instead of a sister. I learned early that women could be the sharpest weapons of all—what I now call the sister wound and the witch wound. These early violences braided themselves into my DNA, creating patterns I would repeat for decades.

I searched for my missing father in every man I met, and found versions of my mother's pain instead. Controlling voices, manipulative hands, dangerous tempers. I stayed too long in relationships that left marks on my body and spirit because being chosen—even poorly—felt better than being alone. One relationship escalated to the point where I was stabbed, yet I survived, carrying both the scar and the shame of why I had stayed.

Through it all, there was a whisper: *You are meant for more.*

That whisper pulled me toward medicine. I became an EMT and spent ten years on ambulances, cradling other people's most raw moments—blood, sweat, prayers, and the metallic tang of emergency rooms. I learned how to press my palms to still chests and beg breath to stay. That work filled me with purpose but also hollowed me in ways I couldn't name. Trauma settled into my bones like an old map—I could navigate crisis, but I had lost my own coordinates.

When COVID came, I wanted to do more. I became a nurse to be the steady presence I'd always needed. But three months into that career, everything I had built was taken from me. My mother had raised me to question vaccinations, and when the hospital mandated the COVID vaccine, I made a choice for my body informed by my history, my family, my beliefs. I said no.

They called me insubordinate. I was fired. My stability—my home, my rhythm, my sense of worth—cracked like glass. I lost my house, nearly lost my car, and at thirty-something I sat in my mother's living room again, carrying humiliation like metal in my mouth. The rooms that had held my childhood grief now held my adult shame.

The darkness that followed was absolute. I felt singled out by the universe, abandoned by systems I had served, shamed by a profession I had devoted myself to. The loneliness became a cavern, and one night, I made a choice that should have been my last. I swallowed pills and felt life unlatch from me like a slow, soft closing of a door. The world dimmed in layers; sound retreated as if someone were turning down the volume of existence.

Then something else came—not noise, but a presence. Ancient, fierce, and tender all at once. A whisper that cut through the dissolving: *Not your time.* My body convulsed as if rejecting the poison of that moment. I vomited violently, like an exorcism of everything I had swallowed. Air returned in ragged, miraculous gasps. I tasted metal and mercy, felt the antiseptic rush of emergency, and knew with stubborn clarity that my story wasn't finished.

That resurrection changed everything. I had been given a second breath, and with it came a dangerous kind of gratitude: survival with responsibility. I owed myself the work of coming back.

Months later, a friend invited me to a breathwork session. I went, hollow and skeptical, but curious about small openings becoming doors. The room was warm; candlelight flickered like a question. We breathed in patterns I had never known—deep, connected rhythms that moved the body's energy and memory.

Breath by breath, something thawed. I cried until my throat was raw—not the shame-filled tears of childhood, but the kind that excavates and leaves space. My chest unclenched like morning frost melting. In those minutes, I met the version of myself who had been waiting: wounded, tender, and impossibly brave. A small ember lodged in my ribs: hope.

Breathwork and Kundalini became my tools of excavation. They gave me keys to rooms I had locked away—the grief room, the abuse room, the womb room. I learned to breathe into trauma and let it move through me instead of staying trapped. Shame that had been tattooed across my days began to dissolve as I practiced exhaling it. I discovered that trauma didn't have to be my destiny—it could be my compost.

Moving to Orlando felt like rebirth. Here, the sister wound began to heal in ways I never imagined possible. Women who might once have been my sharpest edges became my witnesses, my collaborators, my mirrors. Where I had expected competition, I found celebration. The community didn't try to fix me—they reflected me back to myself as whole. In that fertile ground, Luminous Liz was born—not as a persona, but as reclamation.

From there, the work expanded organically. I began leading retreats around the world that felt like coming home to the parts of people who had forgotten how to belong to themselves. These sanctuaries—from Costa Rica in 2026 to locations across the globe—welcome nurses, leaders, practitioners, entrepreneurs, mothers, and CEOs. They serve both women and men who are ready to remember their breath as a portal back to their power. I started certifying teachers in BreathworkDetox, training healers to carry this medicine into hospitals, boardrooms, and the nights when someone feels most alone.

My brand isn't a facade of perfection—it's the map of my recovery. It's the offering of a woman who has fallen apart and rebuilt herself with better tools. I am a traveling nurse by trade and a healer by devotion, a bilingual guide who speaks both the language of clinical care and the language of the sacred.

My mission isn't to fix anyone. It's to create containers where people can locate their voice, feel their bodies, and reclaim their breath, their truth. While I hold specialized spaces for women to reclaim their wombs and feminine essence, my work welcomes all souls ready to heal. I want people to stop apologizing for themselves and know their stories aren't stains—they're scriptures.

Today, I love myself in ways I couldn't have imagined. I lead from places that were once hollow and now hold light. I take people by the hand and remind them of their own breath, because breath remembers how to make room for miracles. I continue my clinical work while also holding the sacred, bridging science and spirit in everything I do.

If there's one line I live by, it's this: *Be the change you wish to see in the world.* I whisper it each morning as prayer and provocation. I spent years learning how to breathe again, and now I spend my life helping others find that return.

If you find yourself in darkness—if your lungs feel like they've forgotten how to take in air—remember there is a way back. There are hands, strangers, and sisters, that will reach. There is breath waiting for you. There is light that, once found, can teach you how to radiate.

You are not your silence. You are not your shame. You are not your trauma.

You are breath. You are power. You are divine.

About Lizbeth

Lizbeth Jimenez—known professionally as Luminous Liz—is a traveling nurse, Master BreathworkDetox facilitator, and founder of the Luminous Healing Collective. Bilingual in English and Spanish, Lizbeth bridges clinical expertise with sacred energy work to lead transformative Breathwork and Kundalini activations, luxury retreats, and teacher certification programs centered on womb healing, somatic release, and embodied empowerment.

Born into generational trauma and raised by a resilient single mother after profound loss, Lizbeth's path is rooted in both service and survival. She spent a decade on ambulances and at the bedside, witnessing life's most fragile moments—experience that informs her trauma-aware, clinically grounded approach to healing. After surviving sexual abuse, domestic violence, and a near-death experience, she channeled her recovery into fierce purpose: creating safe, potent spaces where people can process deep wounds and reclaim their power.

Through her work, Lizbeth is called to inspire and motivate audiences on stages worldwide, helping people see their infinite potential to turn wounds into purpose. She leads retreats internationally, focusing on shadow work for integrative deep healing that transforms pain into passion and trauma into truth. Her offerings include virtual breathwork events, in-person ceremonies, and practitioner certification programs in BreathworkDetox. With a special calling to serve women entrepreneurs and solopreneurs globally, Lizbeth helps them see their infinite light and step into their purpose. She is also expanding her reach to bring healing awareness to hospital systems, ambulance services, fire departments, police forces, and EMS teams, bridging her frontline experience with transformational healing. Her work is celebrated for its raw authenticity, grounded vulnerability, and practical pathways to embodiment.

Lizbeth continues splitting her time between clinical nursing and global facilitation, guided by a simple principle: wounds can become maps, and breath is the path back to self. She leads with lived experience, medical expertise, and luminous commitment to helping everyone heal generational patterns, embody their voice, and step into their full power.

Instagram: @luminouslizllc @toxchemist
Facebook: Lizbeth Jimenez

Becoming HER: The Seed That Needed the Right Environment

Leandrea Long

I could remember the day my life changed. I was filled with fear, overwhelmed by uncertainty. It was the day my older sister told me, "Mom is in the hospital, and she'll be there for a while."

Raised by a single mother, our livelihood hung in the balance. What was supposed to be a routine surgery turned into a near-death situation. During what I thought was a tragedy, God planted the seed of compassion and empathy that would evolve into my life's purpose, helping others regain control of their health and wellness.

Hearing the heart monitor alarm, smelling rubbing alcohol and disinfectant, I could see the nurses and the doctors from where I stood in the hospital's hallway. They asked, "What do you want?" showing no empathy or compassion. The cries for help were ignored. My mother entered the hospital weighing one hundred forty pounds and left weighing only eighty-seven. Still hanging on for dear life, she was skin and bones. How could you treat people this way at the time they need kindness and compassion the most?

That's when I knew I would become someone who'd help restore dignity and not strip it away.

I grew up on the small Caribbean Island of Nassau, The Bahamas. There were not many options, but I knew what I wanted to do with my life. I could recall my sister trying to convince me to go into business, but numbers were never my thing. I was drawn to chemistry, physics, and biology, which became my high school electives.

Once I graduated from high school, my passion led me on an unexpected adventure. I went to Cuba as a foreign exchange student to study pharmacy. The excitement of a new country, learning a new language, and immersing myself in a new culture, quickly turned into homesickness; I was missing family and my comfort zone. After surviving one year, I returned home feeling defeated and disappointed.

Back in Nassau, I worked as a waitress in a local restaurant, making good money, but was frustrated each day by the feeling of defeat still resting in the back of my mind. I was still not in the right environment. I decided to become a nurse, the very profession I'd seen handling my mother without compassion.

I knew I could make a difference—but not confined to that twenty-one-by-seven-mile island. To step into my destiny, I had to leave my comfort zone. This time, I was America-bound and accompanied by my sister. I was determined not to get homesick again; fueled by determination, failure was not an option.

Arriving in America, I was filled with jitteriness and excitement, but also uncertainty. I clung to my mother's words, God's words, which gave me confidence: "You are the head and not the tail, above always and never beneath, a lender and not a borrower," (Deuteronomy 28:13). I enrolled in the Bethune-Cookman University nursing program with funding for one semester and a hope that God would make a way.

Every semester was a struggle to pay tuition, rent, and utilities. Some days, I went without food. I credit working in the admissions office, applying for every scholarship I could, and Mrs. Byrd, who became like a second mother. She provided food, not realizing her generosity was sustaining me. The seed was rooted so deeply that it had to weather the storms for the purpose of manifesting.

God was guiding me to become HER. After two and a half years of weathering nursing school, I struggled with tuition; again, all my resources had dried up. I was at a crossroads. I prayed to God: *You didn't bring me this far to have me fail now.* Failure and defeat crept into my mind once again.

One Sunday morning, the preacher was teaching us about having faith that God can change a person's situation. The message spoke so directly to me that I felt my body shaking, and a waterfall of tears streamed down my face. The pastor said, "I want everyone to get into the aisles, take some change out of your pocket and place it on the ground, as you walk around on the change, have faith that God is going to change your situation."

Hope filled my spirit. With my body still shaking and tears flowing, I knew in my heart that God would come through for me.

A few days later, I stood anxiously in the registrar's line, hoping I wouldn't get embarrassed that I hadn't paid my tuition. When I got to the front of the line, I reluctantly handed over my ID. After a few minutes, the registrar said, "Your classes are all set." Shocked, I figured it had to be a glitch, but at least I didn't have to take the walk of shame to student accounts just yet.

When the first day of classes arrived, I sat in class, nervous and filled with fear that they would find out that I didn't make a payment. When my professor introduced herself and class got started, I breathed a sigh of relief that I was safe. Ten minutes went by, and then came a knock on the door. The person said, "Leandrea Long, you're needed in the dean's office." My heart started beating a million miles an hour. Sweating nervously, I packed up all my belongings, assuming that they'd found out. Embarrassed, I now had to take the walk of shame.

At the dean's office, I braced myself. "Do you know that you were awarded the McPhilps scholarship for the year?" Shocked, I said, "Can you repeat that?" She said it again. Then, I answered, "No." I had never applied for this scholarship, and never heard of it. I cried openly, realizing that God had changed my situation. The remainder of my college would not be a burden anymore. I believed in God. I graduated *summa cum laude* with a bachelor's degree in nursing, debt-free. He made sure the seed was in the right environment to begin to bloom.

More than two decades of caring for others as a nurse went by. Compassion and empathy drove every one of my patient encounters. But as years went by, no one told me of the long hours, the back pain from lifting patients, the mental strain, or skipped meals; it all took its toll. I needed a change from bedside nursing but didn't want to give up on my dream of helping others.

I wanted more—but I wanted to do it in a way that would preserve myself and my passion for helping others. Determined, I ended up earning a master's degree as a clinical nurse leader and a post-master's certificate as a family nurse practitioner, where I would help others as a provider.

With every new milestone, there is a cost. As a mother and wife, balancing my passion and family became difficult. I felt stuck like a caged bird and like there was more for me to do. COVID was the final straw. I was burnt out; it was time for a new seed, the seed of entrepreneurship.

I felt full of excitement again, hope and joy, but overwhelmed by uncertainty, doubt, and fear of failure. I was quietly quitting and planning my exit strategy while nurturing my side hustle, L.A. Wellness Center. I cared for lymphedema patients and post-operative clients, and I coached others to advocate for their physical health.

This new seed couldn't survive in the environment it was in; it was toxic. I remember driving home one night, exhausted from working twelve hours, feet throbbing, an empty stomach, and the heaviness of a surgeon's temper tantrum weighing on my nervous system. For months, I wrestled with the decision of leaving my job.

The weight finally broke me. Sobbing at the steering wheel, hoping that the person in the car next to me didn't notice, I said, "God, it's me again. I need you to tell me what to do because I can't do this anymore."

That following weekend, I received a call from an old co-worker who I hadn't spoken to in a year. I listened as she updated me on her life, then with a brief pause, she said, "Don't be afraid to take the leap, God is with you." I'd been standing in my garage, hiding from the children, and I didn't want them to see me crying. My legs were weak, and I bent over, clutching the phone. God had sent her to answer my petition. It was time to leave my comfort zone yet again so the seed could grow.

My journey was never just about survival; it was about becoming HER. The girl who once stood in a hospital hallway questioning cruelty had blossomed into the woman leading with compassion. The student who once wept over unpaid tuition had become a debt-free graduate, walking in faith. The nurse who once felt trapped by burnout had transformed into an entrepreneur, nurturing others while reclaiming her peace.

My story is proof that seeds need the right soil to thrive. They may endure storms, drought, and darkness, but with faith, resilience, and the courage to step outside of comfort zones, growth always comes. My encouragement to others is simple yet profound: place your seed in the right environment. Protect it, nourish it, and trust the process. Even when storms rage and obstacles loom, never give up. In the right environment, the seed will not just survive, it will flourish and bear fruit.

About Leandrea

Originally from The Bahamas, Leandrea Long is the youngest of three children. She has a sister, Tiffany, and brother, Timothy, and was raised by a single mother, Sharon, who instilled in all of her children to always trust God. Moving to America was a bold move, one sparked by determination and a passion to pursue a dream to be a positive face in healthcare.

Leandrea is a multistate licensed telehealth provider, board-certified family nurse practitioner, and a certified lymphedema therapist. With over two decades of experience in health care, she's brought her expertise to her community, providing concierge medical and aesthetic services dedicated to helping others control their swelling, guiding post-operative patients through recovery, and empowering others to advocate for their physical health. She is changing the lymphedema world by becoming the only advanced practice registered nurse who is also a woman of color, providing lymphedema mobile services in Orlando. She brings therapy directly to the patient, making it more accessible.

Leandrea is passionate about making a positive impact within her community, serving as the director of marketing for Women On The Rise, a women's empowerment group, a mentor for The Greatest Investment Girls Empowerment group, a member of Black Nurses Rock Orlando, and a member of her local church's medical response team.

An entrepreneur at heart, she co-owns a food truck called FedUp BBQ with her husband, Jeyghson. Happily married for fifteen years, they have two daughters, Riley and Marley, who have become a part of her "why." A firm believer in Jesus, she is on a journey to fulfill her divine assignment.

www.leandrealong.com
Instagram: lawellnesscenterllc, leandrea_long
Facebook: leandrealong, l.a.wellnesscenter llc
LinkedIn: Leandrea Long
TickTok: lawellnesscenter

Strength in the Struggle: Building Body Construct and Building Myself

Lori-Ann Marchese

When I first dreamed of opening Body Construct, I never imagined how many battles would come with building a business from the ground up. The vision was simple: create a space for women where they could feel strong, confident, and unstoppable. But what I quickly learned was that success is never handed to you—it is built through trial, error, failure, and getting back up even when the world expects you to stay down.

The Struggles of Starting Something Bigger Than Me

When Body Construct opened its doors, I thought my biggest challenge would be creating workouts that transformed women's bodies. What I didn't anticipate was how many people would doubt me. Some in the community dismissed me as just "a pretty face trying to make money." They couldn't see that my mission was to help women believe in themselves, to show them that confidence and strength could be built one rep, one class, and one positive thought at a time.

I'll never forget one of my earliest encounters with negativity. In the very beginning, when I only had five customers, one of them looked me in the eye and said, "Stop promoting yourself. You're not even worth a dollar." Those words cut deeply, but instead of letting them destroy me, I made myself a promise in that moment: one day she would look back and regret ever saying that. And today, I know she does. Because now, everywhere she looks, she can see the growth, the success, and the power of what I have built.

The truth is, my program was fantastic and the results were incredible. Clients were not only losing weight, but they were gaining strength, confidence, and a sense of belonging. Word of mouth began to spread—those who believed in me shared their success with others, and slowly, a circle of women who truly valued Body Construct began to grow.

I also learned something critical along the way: you cannot put your mindset into the hands of people who are negative, toxic, or just want to bring you and your business down. Another business owner once told me, "You don't even want those kinds of customers. You want the ones who lift you up and believe in your purpose. Your product and your mission will always show through." That wisdom became a guiding light for me.

The road wasn't glamorous. There were months I questioned how I would keep the doors open. I failed more times than I can count—whether it was with programming, financial struggles, or simply trying to convince people that my vision mattered. But every time I failed, I learned. Every time I fell, I got back up. Those battles forged the businesswoman and trainer I am today.

The Media Spotlight and Its Shadow

Along my journey, incredible opportunities came my way: competing in the WBFF World Championship, where I placed in the top three in the world; being crowned Mrs. Connecticut America; landing the cover of *Muscle & Fitness Hers*; and even stepping onto national television as part of Bravo TV's *Game of Crowns*. These were pinch-me moments that represented years of dedication, but they also came with their own set of struggles.

When I appeared on Bravo, my life changed overnight. Suddenly, I wasn't just Lori-Ann the trainer—I was Lori-Ann the TV personality. Instead of boosting my business, that spotlight caused seventy-five percent of my clients to walk away, believing I had become "too Hollywood." The very platform that was meant to elevate me nearly broke me.

I could have quit right there. Many people told me it would be easier to close my doors, leave the cameras behind, and find another path. But something inside of me refused to give up. I knew that if I could survive this storm, the recognition from national TV would eventually open doors. So, I held on tight and rode the wave.

And I was right. Over time, the media exposure that nearly cost me my business began to bring people back—clients who once doubted me started to believe again, and new opportunities emerged that I could never have created alone. Bravo TV taught me the hardest lesson: sometimes, your biggest challenges disguise your biggest blessings.

Learning to Ignore the Noise

With growth also came resistance. I remember receiving a phone call from a person in another state—nearly three hours away— demanding I remove my logo from my business name. It was trademarked, but I was nervous when they said they were getting a lawyer. So I removed it. They saw how Body Construct was rising, and they felt threatened by my success. To me, that moment said everything. If someone that far away was bothered by my name, it meant Body Construct had power. It meant my brand was making waves.

That experience reinforced something I had already started to learn: hate thrives on reaction. Haters want a response, but the best thing you can do is ignore them and keep moving forward. After that incident, I stopped wasting energy on negativity and poured everything into the women who believed in me, trusted me, and wanted results.

And those results spoke for themselves. My clients' transformations were televised locally and nationally. They were featured in *Muscle & Fitness Hers* magazine spreads. They were talked about on TV segments and highlighted in print features. The proof of my program silenced the doubters—because no matter how much hate came my way, the truth was undeniable: Body Construct worked.

I realized something powerful: people can hate you, misunderstand you, or try to bring you down—but if your results are undeniable, eventually, everyone comes around.

Finding Strength in the Face of Doubt

What I've learned over these years is that your mindset is everything. Success doesn't just depend on talent, or resources, or even luck—it depends on resilience. There were moments when even my closest friends or family didn't understand the sacrifices I was making. There were times when clients questioned me or turned away. But if I had listened to every voice of doubt, Body Construct would have been a memory instead of the thriving community it is today.

I often remind myself and my clients: you cannot allow anyone—whether it's family, friends, or customers—to determine your destiny. If you know your purpose, you have to keep moving forward, no matter who tries to stand in your way.

Gratitude for the Struggle

Today, I look back at all the battles—the financial stress, the criticism, the loss of clients, the long hours, the self-doubt—and I realize those were the very things that shaped me. Without them, I wouldn't have developed the strength to stand tall in an industry that is not always kind to women.

The truth is, being on Bravo, gracing magazine covers, and holding titles all gave me credibility. But more than that, they gave me grit. The same media that brought negativity also gave me opportunities I'll forever be grateful for. Doors opened that I never could have imagined—opportunities that allowed me to inspire, teach, and build a platform bigger than I ever dreamed.

Through my eyes and through my battles, I now see the payoff. I am traveling and training women virtually across the nation. I am being invited to do workouts at major wellness and health events, sharing my journey and expertise. People recognize my value and my worth, and they see my passion shining through every award, every title, and every piece of recognition. And the best part is this: today, the work is finding me.

The Lesson I Carry Forward

If there's one message I want to share through *Slaying Orlando*, it's this: success is not about never falling. Success is about how many times you get back up when life knocks you down. It's about fighting for your vision even when the people closest to you can't see it. It's about staying true to your purpose even when the world doubts you.

I built Body Construct not just as a gym, but as a movement—a place where women could rise together. And though my path has been filled with struggles, I wouldn't change any of it. Because every battle has prepared me for the woman, the entrepreneur, and the leader I am today.

As I continue this journey, I hold on to one simple truth: strength doesn't come from easy victories. It comes from staying in the fight, even when the odds are against you. And for that, I am grateful—for the struggle, for the resilience, and for the chance to keep rising, stronger than before.

About Lori-Ann

Lori-Ann Marchese is a globally recognized fitness expert, nutrition coach, and entrepreneur known for her powerful, results-driven approach to women's wellness through mind, body, and soul transformation. She is the founder and owner of Body Construct, an all-women's gym in Connecticut that has been empowering women for over fifteen years.

Lori-Ann offers virtual training programs and travels nationwide for exclusive personal training, bringing her signature coaching and energy to clients wherever they are. Her personalized approach, whether online or in-person, is designed to meet women exactly where they are and guide them toward lasting strength, health, and confidence.

Crowned Mrs. Connecticut America, Lori-Ann rose to national fame as a cast member on Bravo TV's *Game of Crowns* and continues to be a leading media personality. She has been featured on Great Day Connecticut (WFSB News) and in top media outlets, including ET!, *OK! Magazine*, *Star Magazine*, and *Muscle & Fitness Hers*, where she has also appeared on the cover. She was named one of the Top Trainers in the World by *Huffington Post New York*.

Lori-Ann is also a contributor to *Bella Magazine*, where she shares fitness, beauty, and mindset expertise. Through her media presence, gym community, and elite coaching, she continues to inspire women to become their strongest selves—inside and out.

www.BodyConstructFitness.com
Instagram: @bcgymct @loriann.marchese

The Light Side of Leadership

Lady Alisha Martin

At twenty-two years old, I filed for bankruptcy. I didn't come from wealth or privilege. I grew up poor, and what I inherited wasn't money but the unhealthy financial habits of survival. Credit cards, debt, and the idea that money slips through your fingers faster than you can hold it. That was the reality I learned at home. Filing for bankruptcy so young felt like I had failed at adulthood before I had even begun. I thought the road ahead of me had already closed.

But instead of accepting that cycle, I made a decision to break it. I knew if I ever wanted a different life, I had to understand the one thing that had always controlled mine: money. I figured the best way to learn it and make sure I never ended up in that position again was to make it my career. So I got into banking.

I threw myself into the work. I learned everything I could about credit, savings, budgeting, and the psychology of money. I worked hard to pay my bills, chipped away at the debt, and little by little began to rebuild my credit. For the first time, I felt a sense of control, stability, and momentum. I could almost see that elusive 800 credit score within reach—proof that I had not only changed my circumstances but rewritten my story.

And then, in an instant, everything changed.

We were in a devastating, near-fatal car accident that shattered everything. It upended the life I had fought so hard to rebuild.

My neck and back were broken. For the next five years, I lived confined to a bed. The doctors told me I would never walk again without aid, that my life would require assistance from here on out. I underwent seventeen surgeries, dealt with permanent nerve damage, PTSD, depression, and a pain so constant and unrelenting that some days, surviving the next sixty seconds felt impossible. At one point, the only option offered was to live with a morphine pump installed in my body.

I couldn't be the wife, the friend, or the professional I wanted to be. I couldn't even be the version of myself I thought I was supposed to be. The despair was suffocating, and there were days when I wondered if life was worth continuing. But somewhere in that darkness, I realized that resilience doesn't mean being untouched by pain; it means deciding what to do with it. I knew what I had been doing the last five years wasn't working, so it was time to try something else.

I began to think of those years as what I now call my "Black Bow Gifts," life-changing opportunities disguised as disasters, wrapped in packaging no one would ever choose. They come to us looking like bankruptcy, heartbreak, illness, or loss, but inside them lies the chance to reinvent ourselves. And that's what I did.

Less than a year after changing my mindset, I started finding real solutions. On 11/11/11 (my "Bionic Birthday"), I received two implanted neurostimulation machines and batteries designed to help manage the pain without any pharmaceuticals or "drugs." It didn't fully erase the pain, but it gave me something more important: another chance at life. I could walk again. I could, figuratively and literally, finally move forward. Now that I could get out of bed, I wasn't just going to walk across the room, I was going to dance across EVERY room. I immediately began trying to make up for the five years that were lost.

Those years I was confined to my bed taught me lessons no classroom could have. I learned that every moment counts, that when life feels unbearable, you can focus on getting through the next sixty seconds. I learned that perspective is power. You don't always get to choose your circumstances, but you always get to choose your outlook. And I learned that joy is medicine. Laughter wasn't a distraction from pain; it was the antidote. Those lessons became the blueprint not only for my personal healing but for how I would eventually show up in leadership.

I had a realization that stopped me in my tracks. If I could do that with my own life, what else could this mindset work on? I started looking at my team and saw the same patterns I'd once lived through. People were weighed down, avoiding hard things, letting negativity take the lead. It reminded me too much of my own darkness, and I knew there was a better way. So I decided to bring what had healed me into the workplace. If I could transform pain into progress, maybe I could transform burnout into belonging, dread into drive, and exhaustion into joy.

At first, the impact wasn't immediate, far from it. Most of the employees didn't want to participate. They rolled their eyes, made jokes, and thought I was ridiculous for trying to make work "fun." They were miserable, and honestly, I couldn't blame them. But I had already lived through the unimaginable, and I wasn't going back there again. Not even for a visit. So I made a decision: even if everyone around me was miserable, I was still going to have fun. I was going to find the joy no matter what. I started leaning into it even more, especially on the hardest days. I'd crank up the energy, add a silly theme, or bring in something unexpected just to trick my own brain into looking forward to the day instead of dreading it. And slowly but surely, it started to work. People started to get excited about what was going to happen next. One by one, the attitudes began to shift. Call-outs and burnout dropped.

Our customer service improved, our sales grew, and suddenly people were saying things like, "You have the best job in the world," and, "Do you even work? It looks like you're always having fun." What they didn't realize was that the fun wasn't the absence of work, the fun WAS the work. Joy became our culture, and results naturally followed.

The philosophy that saved me in my darkest days became the philosophy that transformed my career. Bankruptcy at twenty-two gave me empathy and humility, and it fueled my passion for helping others find financial wellness and learning from my mistakes. The wheelchair gave me resilience, proof that progress doesn't have to be perfect and that persistence matters more than appearances. And using my creativity gave me the courage to turn pain into purpose and hard work into joy.

When I look back, I don't regret the bankruptcy, the pain, or even the years I was bedridden. I wouldn't erase them if I could. They gave me a unique mindset at a very young age. They gave me the perspective that hardship isn't the end of the story, but often the beginning of a new one. My worst days became the foundation of a winning philosophy.

Today, I bring with me the lessons that were carved out of disaster. I bring the conviction that leadership is a conscious choice, that every day we can decide to curate a great day not only for ourselves but for our teams. I bring the belief that the Light Side of Leadership isn't about pretending everything is easy. It's about meeting the hardest moments with creativity, humor, and optimism.

I went from bankruptcy to the boardroom, from despair to purpose, not because the road was easy, but because I chose to see every setback as a Black Bow Gift. The light I found in those moments is the same light I now try to share with every team I lead, every partnership I build, and every challenge I face.

And if there's one truth my journey has taught me, it's this: the light is always there. You just have to choose to see it...and then choose to lead with it.

About Alisha

Lady Alisha Martin is proof that resilience wears heels. As the vice president of business and economic development at Suncoast Credit Union, she leads with strategy, creativity, and an almost suspicious amount of enthusiasm for networking and community impact. Known for turning obstacles into opportunities, she's built a reputation as the woman who can walk into any room and make *everyone* feel like they belong there.

A published author, award-winning leader, and visionary maverick, Lady Alisha combines almost three decades of experience in business development, community support, and financial empowerment with a dash of humor and a whole lot of heart. Her latest chapter—literally—was being featured as a co-author in the inspiring book *Slaying Naples*, celebrating powerhouse women and their stories of grit and growth.

When she's not helping businesses and communities thrive, you can find her building connections that matter, mentoring emerging leaders, or crafting jewelry that somehow doubles as a networking tool. (Yes, she's been known to close a deal while wearing a statement necklace that *she made herself.*)

She's a true survivor of life's plot twists (including a comeback story that starts in a wheelchair and ends in a boardroom) and self-proclaimed "serial connector." Lady Alisha Martin continues to prove that purpose, passion, and a good sense of humor are the ultimate power trio.

Instagram: @thelishmartin

Beyond the Runway: When Style, Story, and Compassion Walk Hand in Hand

Josie NeJame

The lights dimmed at Rosen Shingle Creek hotel, and the music rose as the applause grew louder and louder while one hundred twenty children battling pediatric cancer walked the runway. Some held the hands of celebrities and their doctors, some carried signs, and others moved on their own with the confidence of seasoned models. These children were fighters. Some had bald heads and scars, their tiny frames sometimes marked by tubes and ports, yet their smiles were radiant, and their laughter was infectious. As they walked in the annual Runway to Hope Soirée, the crowd of 2,480 supporters rose to their feet, clapping with tears of joy streaming, hearts breaking and mending all at once. That moment was more than just a fashion show. It was a reminder that hope is not fragile. Hope is powerful, resilient, and alive. In that moment, I knew what we had created was not just another event; it was a movement.

Giving back has always been a part of me. Although I was not born in Orlando like the rest of my family, this city has always been home. It has given me some of my greatest loves: family, friendships, and a community that believes in showing up for one another. Giving back has always been a part of me. When my husband Mark and I founded Runway to Hope in 2010, it was not because cancer had struck our own family. It was because we listened to parents in our community who told us that their child was happy and healthy until one day a bruise appeared, a fever lingered, or a blood test revealed a word no parent should ever have to hear: *cancer*.

We quickly realized that we often had said the same things regarding our daughters, Valentina and Alessandra, that we were grateful that they were happy and healthy. We understood that you do not have to wait until tragedy touches your doorstep to create change. You do not have to have a child with cancer to know the devastation it brings to a family. You only have to listen to the stories of parents whose entire lives were turned upside down in a single moment. Their child had been running in the yard, laughing at dinner, teasing their siblings. Then suddenly, hospital rooms replaced playgrounds, chemotherapy replaced soccer practice, and fear replaced certainty.

We knew we could not take away their diagnosis, but we could step into their story. We could create a platform for these children to be celebrated and for their families to know they were not alone. At Runway to Hope, we have believed from the very beginning that no family should battle pediatric cancer alone. Our vision was that through relationships built within our community, Runway to Hope would foster collaborative efforts among hospitals, corporations, businesses, philanthropists, corporations, and families raising funds and awareness. We hoped this would bring new programs and initiatives to the pediatric cancer community, while providing direct support and aid primarily to Central Florida children and their families.

We also hoped to bring new or underserved medical programs and initiatives to the Central Florida pediatric cancer community and also provide direct support and aid to the families through our Family Assistance Program.

This Family Assistance Program would help with mortgages, gas, groceries, and sometimes even the unthinkable costs of end-of-life care. We would show up during the darkest moments and remain beside them.

At Runway to Hope, we have done all that we had hoped for—and continue to do so today.

These stories do not belong to me. They belong to the families who shared them, but I am their witness—and because of that, I am forever changed. Runway to Hope has become a tapestry woven from thousands of threads: three major hospitals, doctors and nurses, elected officials, media outlets, designers, corporate partners, volunteers, and an entire community willing to rally for one cause. The children are the stars of the show, but the story is collective. It is the story of Orlando at its best, and of humanity at its most compassionate. Healing does not always mean a cure. Sometimes it is a burst of laughter in the middle of fear, a night when a child feels like a superhero, or a memory created in the middle of a battle.

After more than a decade immersed in the stories of pediatric cancer families, I came to another realization. Storytelling was not only the heartbeat of Runway to Hope. It was the heartbeat of everything I did. That realization led me to explore my writing and then into my next chapter, WTFJosie! People laugh when they first hear the name, and they ask what it stands for. The acronym is intentional: it means *wellness, travel, and fashion*. These are three threads of my life that create joy, inspiration, and connection in the lives of others. And yes, I'll admit, I do love a good curse word now and then. The name makes me laugh because it captures both sides of me: the one who writes about Paris Fashion Week and wellness rituals, and the other who believes life is too short not to laugh, curse a little, and keep things real.

At first glance, some might wonder how wellness tips or stories from Paris Fashion Week could exist beside the raw stories of pediatric cancer families. But to me, it's the same instinct expressed differently. Stories of wellness remind us how to heal body, mind, and soul. Stories of travel invite us to wonder, to remember that the world is wide and full of possibility. Stories of fashion remind us to dream, to embrace creativity, to find confidence and self-expression. Just as Runway to Hope has given children a platform to shine, WTF Josie gives me a platform to inspire and connect. It is lighter, yes, but no less meaningful because inspiration itself is a kind of medicine. At first, I thought of Runway to Hope and WTF Josie as two separate paths, one rooted in philanthropy and the other in lifestyle. The more I leaned into both, the more I realized they were connected by the same thread: storytelling.

Runway to Hope heals through stories. WTF Josie inspires through stories. Together, they remind me that storytelling is one of the most powerful tools we have. Stories create empathy. When a family shares the heartbreak of a diagnosis, we are moved to compassion. When someone shares a travel experience or a moment of wellness, we are reminded that joy is possible. Stories spark change. Runway to Hope raises funds for pediatric cancer support, but its true impact is in the way it shifts lives. WTF Josie, in a different way, encourages us to live with intention, beauty, and connection.

Stories celebrate life, whether it is a child in remission walking the runway or a quiet moment in a café in Paris. Stories remind us that life is worth living fully. If there is one lesson my journey has taught me, it is that we do not always get to choose our stories. A diagnosis comes. A job changes. A dream shifts. Life interrupts. But we do get to choose whether we share our stories. When we share them honestly, with compassion and courage, something extraordinary happens. Healing begins. Inspiration takes root. Communities grow stronger.

For me, storytelling has always been my way of giving back. Through Runway to Hope, I have witnessed the fierce courage of children and families. Through my writing, I have been able to share joy, beauty, and imagination with the world. Both are part of my legacy. Both are part of who I am. If I could leave you with one thought, it would be this: tell your story. Whether it is about partnership or hope, about fashion or fear, about travel or trial, tell it. Someone out there needs to hear your words so they can find healing in them, and so another will be inspired to keep going because you shared a piece of your truth.

Stories remind us to keep dreaming, keep healing, and keep celebrating life. Because stories heal. Stories inspire. And our stories, told with heart, can change the world.

About Josie

Josie NeJame is the co-founder of Runway to Hope, a nonprofit dedicated to supporting children and families impacted by pediatric cancer. Together with her husband, attorney Mark NeJame, she received the Lifetime Achievement Award in philanthropy from the AFP for their enduring impact on the Orlando community. Her leadership and influence have also been recognized in the city's prestigious list of the 50 Most Powerful in Orlando, and she is an Emmy award-winning producer.

Beyond her professional and philanthropic achievements, she is most proud of being a mother to her two daughters, Valentina and Alessandra. Josie balances family with a passion for writing for a local magazine, where she shares stories of fashion, travel, and wellness, often from the front rows of Paris Fashion Week or while exploring destinations around the globe. She is also the founder of WTF Josie, a lifestyle platform dedicated to wellness, travel, and fashion, where she continues to share her vision and entrepreneurial spirit.

Whether on the runway, in a feature story, or through her nonprofit work, she blends elegance, authenticity, and heart, all while inspiring others to dream, heal, and connect.

Instagram: @josienejame
www.wtfjosie.com
www.runwaytohope.org

From Smiles to Styles: Mom, Wife, Entrepreneur–One Manicure at a Time

Kasia Pukeca

Imagine going to college, working in the dental field—a specialized, respected profession—climbing your way up to a great position and feeling like you've made it. You did what was expected. You followed the plan. A few years later, you get married, have three kids close in age, and check off another box on life's accomplishment list. Everything looks perfect on paper.

But then, the routine starts to weigh on you. You feel the "Sunday Scaries" every week—that sinking sense of dread before Monday. You realize the spark is missing.

I knew deep down this couldn't be the end of my story. I was bored—and boredom doesn't mix well with a creative brain that's always searching for new ways to express itself. As a lifelong creative (with a sprinkle of ADD), I knew I needed something more stimulating. Years before this realization, I had an idea tucked in the back of my mind: *I want to open a nail salon.* But not just any salon—one I would actually want to go to.

For a long time, I ignored that thought. I had already done the school thing, earned my degree, and established a stable career. Was I really going to start all over again? What would my family think?

It wasn't that I hated dentistry—I didn't. It just wasn't fulfilling. I started noticing that the moments I felt truly happy were when I was doing something creative. That nagging idea of a nail salon kept resurfacing, and I finally accepted that it wasn't going away.

I spent months thinking about whether I was ready to take the leap, and the more I thought about it, the clearer it became: this was meant for me. Interestingly, as I began mapping out my vision for this new business, I realized that many skills from dentistry naturally aligned with what I wanted to create.

My extensive training in sterilization and sanitation—ensuring patient safety and health—became a foundational pillar for how I envisioned the salon. I was passionate about attention to detail and creating comfortable, meticulous experiences for clients. I loved working with my hands—whether fabricating crowns and mouthguards or removing orthodontic appliances to reveal a perfect smile.

As I researched the nail industry and learned about products and techniques, everything started to click. This new dream combined precision, care, and creativity—everything I loved. It was decided.

Motherhood and Motivation

Motherhood shaped me as much as dentistry did. When I first opened my one-woman nail studio, I poured my heart, soul, and every ounce of energy into building my brand. I worked long, demanding days filled with clients, often skipping lunch breaks just to fit in one more appointment. Then I'd head home to handle admin work, all while being a wife and mom to three little ones.

I did this for years. Eventually, I hit a wall. The burnout was real. I realized this wasn't sustainable—not for me or anyone else. That's when a new vision began forming: *a salon culture that truly supported work-life balance.*

I knew I couldn't do it alone. I needed a team. And I wanted that team to thrive. So, I made the decision to hire employees instead of contractors. This way, they'd have stable pay, consistent schedules, and an environment that supported a healthy life outside of work.

I wanted my technicians to be able to clock out and *truly* be done for the day—not worrying about messages or bookings at home. Our system was designed so that time off didn't mean guilt, and clients could still be cared for by another trained team member. Communication and collaboration became core values.

We also built a structure that supported both clients and staff: extended hours for last-minute nail breaks, team training to ensure consistent quality, and most importantly, a culture rooted in empathy and respect.

Being a mom taught me time management, the value of relationships, and how vital it is to carve out time for yourself.

Those lessons became the foundation of Gloss—a business that cares equally for its team and its clients.

Starting Small and Dreaming Big

Starting a business completely solo was one of the scariest things I've ever done. I took it slowly. After enrolling in nail school, getting licensed, purchasing products, and creating a business plan, I began humbly—from home.

That phase was essential. It gave me time to refine my craft, test products, learn from mistakes, and build consistency. I didn't have rent looming over my head yet, so I could focus on quality.

Then, word started spreading. Referrals came in. I reached a point where I could confidently afford a professional space, and that's when I made the leap. It was terrifying, but necessary. The small overhead was gone, replaced by rent and bigger responsibilities. I worked relentlessly—long, packed days with no breaks, juggling motherhood and entrepreneurship.

When the kids were asleep, I'd dive into admin work, inventory management, and social media—my least favorite part. I've never been naturally tech-savvy, but I had to learn quickly. If I wanted my business to grow, I had to show up online, share my story, and connect with people.

All that effort started to pay off. My schedule filled up, and my waitlist kept growing. One day, my husband asked, "So how many people are on your waitlist now?" I counted over three hundred names. That was the moment we both knew: it was time to expand.

I was maxed out on time, energy, and capacity. Growth required help. So, I hired my first employee—an admin. Kamri joined the team, and from the moment we met, I knew she understood the vision. She believed in what we were building, and she's still with Gloss today.

Opening Gloss

On November 1, 2023, Gloss officially opened its doors. I'll never forget that week—the most stressful Halloween of my life. Between trick-or-treating with my three kids and preparing to launch a brand-new business, I was stretched to my limits.

With a team of eight and a much larger overhead, the stakes were higher than ever. It wasn't just my paycheck on the line anymore—it was everyone's. That pressure was immense.

But through the chaos came clarity. Every challenging moment had taught me something. The harder the time, the stronger and more confident I became—not just as a business owner, but as a mom and wife too.

One of the biggest challenges was figuring out how to communicate the *value* of what we were doing. Gloss was unlike any other nail salon in the area. We weren't competing on price; we were redefining standards. That meant we had to educate clients on why our approach mattered: proper sterilization, consistent training, ethical pay, and an elevated experience that prioritized health and artistry.

Many people doubted it could work. Some said it was impossible to build a sustainable business at a higher price point. There were plenty of negative comments. But I knew my "why"— and it was strong enough to push through the noise.

I wanted to create something better for both clients and technicians, and I wasn't going to compromise that vision. Over time, the message began to spread. People started understanding the difference, and positivity replaced doubt.

Looking Forward

Today, Gloss continues to grow—and so do I. The comfort zone doesn't excite me anymore. Growth does. I am now much more well-equipped to handle pressures. I avoid hard tasks less and less, and I'm more excited to learn what will be on the other side as I rise through it.

That's why I'm thrilled to share that we're working on Gloss 2.0, opening soon in Lake Nona. It's more than just a new location; it's an evolution. A space designed to build community, support creativity, and maintain everything we stand for—excellence, safety, artistry, and balance.

This move also aligns perfectly with my family's next chapter. We're relocating to Lake Nona to support my kids in their soccer journeys, while I continue mine as a business owner and leader.

Looking back, I wouldn't change a thing. Every late night, every doubt, every moment of exhaustion—it all led to this. Gloss isn't just a salon; it's a reflection of growth, resilience, and passion. It's proof that it's never too late to rewrite your story.

About Kasia

Kasia Pukeca is a brick-and-mortar business owner supporting a team, a wife, and a mother of three energetic, sports-loving children. She balances the chaos of family life, travel soccer schedules, and marriage with the demands of entrepreneurship. She has created a luxury nail business that redefines the salon experience for both clients and team members.

After not being able to find a nail salon that met her personal standards for cleanliness, service, and aesthetic, Kasia took matters into her own hands and created a high-end nail studio with intention, care, and quality in mind. As a previous registered dental hygienist, her standards were way above what the current market was offering.

Her studio is built with meticulous dry manicure techniques, fume-free services, and medical-grade sterilization protocols. Only professional tools and clean, high-quality products are used, ensuring every client receives the safest and most sophisticated experience possible. Beyond just the client experience, Kasia has created a supportive and empowering work environment for her team. All staff receive extensive training and ongoing education and are treated as true professionals within a career and growth focused setting, a rarity in the industry.

Married to a fellow entrepreneur, Norbert Pukeca, she understands the value of hard work and taking a risk and is very supportive in her business ventures while being an equal partner when it comes to parenting and being present for their children. Her dedication to excellence, family, and community is evident in every aspect of her business. She continues to be an inspiration to other women seeking to build businesses that reflect their values without compromising on quality, health, or happiness.

Instagram: gloss.nailco & nailsxkash
www.glossnailco.com

Steering from Heaven:
A Daughter's Journey of Love, Loss, and Purpose

Christina Pinto Rogers, CFP®

A New Beginning

We arrived from Cuba on January 20, 1966, to what's known today as the Freedom Tower in Miami, the first stop in our new life. My parents were brave and ready to start over at thirty-two and forty-two, leaving everything behind for a new country. I was too young to understand then, but looking back, that moment shaped who I am and how I face challenges.

We were living in New Jersey. At four years old, I didn't speak English, but I was off to kindergarten to make friends and learn. My dad had lived in New York years earlier, and as a teacher in Cuba, my mom also spoke English. Before long, I did too and now fit in with the advantage of being bilingual.

Watching my parents start over taught me that courage and reinvention are essential. They gave up everything; their locksmith business, a home, friends, and family, to give my brother and me something greater: a safer life in a country full of opportunity and freedom. My dad was the visionary and my mom courageously followed in his footsteps, supporting all of his ideas.

My name is Christina Pinto Rogers, a CERTIFIED FINANCIAL PLANNER®. My first managerial role at sixteen taught me that true respect is earned, not given by a title. College wasn't a traditional experience for me. While my friends were away at school, I worked full-time and attended night classes at Valencia Community College and later University of Central Florida. It taught me discipline early on and prepared me for everything that followed.

After many years in banking, I got the entrepreneurship bug and joined friends at Fortiv, a financial planning firm in downtown Orlando. Leaving a steady paycheck was scary, but I reminded myself that my parents had started over, and if they can do it, so could I. I promised to work hard, keep learning, and always do what's best for my clients.

The Journey That Awakened My Purpose

My dad passed away in 2000, and losing him was incredibly hard. He was my hero, the one who always said, "I don't worry about you because I know that no matter what, you will be fine."

He protected me, made me laugh, and was always there for me. He also believed I me, and I still miss him every day.

My mom was very smart, sweet, and independent. It wasn't until 2008 that my next chapter began. Caregiving doesn't begin when someone is bedridden, it starts quietly, a doctor's appointment here, a bill there, until one day you realize you're keeping everything together for them. It's one of life's most challenging and rewarding roles that no one prepares you for.

We were lucky, she had a long-term care insurance policy, one she didn't want, didn't understand, and didn't want to pay. Every month she'd say, "I'm not talking to you unless you cancel this policy," and I'd say, "Mom, I'm not cancelling it, and you'll thank me one day." When the time came, she did and was grateful to have care at home fully paid for. It saved us emotionally, physically, and financially.

My caregiving years were tough; we had good and bad days. I remember days feeling helpless, starting my morning in tears wondering how I will get through another day. I was single, running my own business, caring for my mother and juggling my own life.

I learned that caring for someone you love means learning to care for yourself too. Even small moments of rest or laughter gave me the strength to keep going.

Giving back to the community through Prospera helped me stay grounded. Serving as statewide and regional chair gave me a renewed sense of purpose, something I desperately needed at that time.

My biggest fear was what would happen to my mom if something happened to me. If I got sick or worse, who would know what to do? I realized I was no longer her daughter; I was the keeper of every detail of her life.

Out of necessity and fear I started organizing all her important personal, legal and medical information into a binder. I didn't know it then, but I was building a version of what is known today as *The Personal Playbook* — an organizational tool that made it easier for others to step in and keep her care consistent. If something happened to me, my niece Chelsea would have everything she needed all in one place. That binder gave me peace of mind when little else did.

As I was spending more time with my mom, I saw parts of her in me, her thoughtfulness, attention to detail and organization. I'd always thought I was just like my dad, but I realized I was like both. She came to depend on me, and I discovered a deeper appreciation for her and loved our time together.

My mom's biggest fears were passing away and that I'd still be single. I told her, "I'm not alone, I have incredible friends and a full life". She would say, "It's not the same as having a partner." My parents were married forty-four years, still holding hands until the day he passed. She knew what companionship meant and wanted the same for me.

The online dating app, Bumble, changed my life because that's where I met Ben. My mom knew he was the one before I did and that he'd be there for me every step of the way.

In 2019, my mom passed away peacefully in her sleep. It was sudden, and I was in shock. Ben and Chelsea were amazing and supported me through heartbreak. The night before, I'd dreamed of her walking away as if to say; my work as a mother is done. I can rest now; you no longer need my protection.

One year later, Ben proposed, and we were married on Valentine's Day 2021. I knew my mom and dad were smiling in heaven, especially my mom.

A Legacy of Love Through Long Term Concierge

Back at the office, something unexpected happened. My clients knew I was caring for my mom and began asking for advice about their parents. I realized that while most people planned carefully for retirement, almost no one planned for caregiving, what to do before or after a crisis. Some companies addressed small pieces of the puzzle, but no one was helping them with the entire picture.

A few months after my mom passed away, I felt a need to keep her memory alive by helping others and sharing all the lessons we had learned. Out of that mix of love, loss, passion, and purpose, *Long Term Concierge* was born. We wanted to make caregiving easier for the next daughter, son, or spouse. That is why we say, "The Greatest Gift is a Plan."

My husband, Ben, encouraged me every step of the way along with my dear friend and executive assistant Leysha, who helped me bring my ideas to life. I couldn't have done it without her by my side. We created a simple one-page diagram placing me at the center, surrounded by the trusted professionals that families needed: an attorney, caregiving agencies, meal deliveries and more. It became the first visual of what I wanted to build, a professional network.

We were ready to launch when the world shut down. COVID delayed everything, but the word spread through friends and clients. Helping families get organized, I realized it wasn't just my mom who struggled with losing her independence, everyone does. It's hard for people to accept help, even when they need it the most.

By 2022 surrounded by family and friends, we officially launched, *Long Term Concierge*. I was proud we had come this far and nervous about what would happen next. Each step so far has felt guided, as if my mom were steering the ship from heaven.

Long Term Concierge continues to grow, and today we offer multiple plans and three versions of the *Personal Playbook*, that organizer I once created for my mom. There's the Seniors edition and now Children's and Singles/Couples too.

Being organized doesn't stop an emergency from happening, but it does make it easier to manage, making better decisions and reducing stress when life feels uncertain. Balancing both businesses isn't always easy, but I wouldn't trade it for anything. I feel blessed every day and I truly believe my mom continues guiding me to the right people at the right time.

As a Hispanic woman and the daughter of entrepreneurial immigrants, I've learned that hard work, faith, and perseverance make anything possible, especially in the United States of America.

My journey is a tribute to my parents' courage, and I hope my story reminds others that even in life's hardest moments, purpose and passion can be found to create something beautiful.

To my family, especially my husband, who has been my rock—thank you for your love and support. And to my parents, whose sacrifices shaped every part of who I am—*Los quiero, mucho, mucho, mucho.*

About Christina

Christina Pinto Rogers, CFP® is the founder of *Long Term Concierge*, where she's redefining how aging seniors and their families prepare for the future—by making the present more manageable. Drawing from her own caregiving journey and her expertise as a CERTIFIED FINANCIAL PLANNER®, Christina blends compassionate support with practical planning to ease the emotional and logistical weight of aging. Her custom framework helps families navigate long-term care, insurance coordination, and essential document organization, while also streamlining everyday decisions through tools like the *Personal Playbook*. Christina's work empowers seniors to age with clarity, dignity, and confidence—thoughtfully addressing both immediate needs and future goals. In doing so, she helps families feel prepared, supported, and uplifted as they navigate the challenges and changes of growing older. We are honored to have Christina in *Slaying Orlando* as she continues her mission to support seniors in our community.

www.longtermconcierge.com
Facebook: Long Term Concierge
Instagram: longtermconcierge
LinkedIn: Long Term Concierge
YouTube: @longtermconcierge

The Fine Art of Estate Sales and Second Chances

Melissa Sullivan

After twenty-five years in IT, I was certain my destiny involved fluorescent lights, bad coffee, and a keyboard-shaped imprint on my face. I never pictured making a living outside corporate America, but now I own Posh Peacock Estate Sales, one of Orlando's largest estate sale companies. Often it doesn't even feel like work—to paraphrase Mark Twain, if you do what you love, you'll never work a day in your life. (You'll just haul vintage lamps at dawn.)

My road to get here was not a straight line. It was more of a detour through cold, ugly cubicles and hours staring at screens—

which is where I would probably still be if not for a near-fatal illness and the clarity it brought.

In 2008, I was living in Seattle with my husband and our six-month-old son when I realized I was in constant low-level pain. Like an annoying bug flying around my face, it was always there. Around that time, my marriage also began to crumble. Caring for an infant, working full-time, and trying to keep my little family intact kept my mind off the pain. Our marriage ended when our son was two, but the pain didn't get the memo. It moved in and brought friends: bone pain in all my limbs, an upset stomach, and an unexpected talent for breaking toes.

Doctors examined me, ran tests, and found—nothing. A physiologist shrugged and offered pain medication. I declined; I'd had bad experiences with side effects and didn't want to trade bone pain for a new personality.

We moved to Florida when my son was four years old to be closer to family. The pain followed, now joined by a persistent brain fog that clouded my once-sharp memory.

More doctors. Their answers ranged from "early menopause" to "drink more water" to the ever-suspicious, "Are you trying to get pain meds?"

No. The answer to that last question was always no. I wanted to know the source of the pain. Plus, I had no history of addiction issues (well, I do love my dessert, but that's a whole other story). I rarely took any pain medication at all, except for an occasional Advil for the toes that I suddenly seemed to be breaking regularly. After hearing the question enough times, I became numb to it and stopped going to doctors completely. I could have been the star of a medical reality show called *Doubt My Suffering*.

In addition to pain, stomach upset, and brain fog, I began getting lost. Not only was my ability to follow a simple map gone, I struggled with simple GPS instructions. Once, I got turned around in the neighborhood, then on trips to the grocery and to my mother's house—both less than a half-mile away. Another time, I got lost walking the dog three blocks from home. I cried in secret because I didn't want my elementary-school-age son to witness his mother's meltdown. I'd managed to fool him about Santa and the Easter Bunny, but I couldn't fool him now. He knew.

By 2018, things worsened. I started passing out. I also took naps that were less "restful lie-down" and more "mysterious vanishing act." Working from home became a safety feature—I couldn't risk keeling over during a status meeting. I don't know that I hid it well from my higher-ups. My performance reviews remained stellar, but coworkers gently inquired about my health. Terrified of being a jobless, single mother, I dodged questions and stayed quiet. I'd seen so many doctors and received no answers except mild insinuations that I was a hypochondriac. Self-doubt crept in, and I started to wonder if I was losing my mind.

Things reached a low point in August 2019. Not only was I passing out, but I was taking up to two naps a day. One afternoon, my son woke me with tears on his face, and he whispered, "I thought you were dead." It was an honest, terrifying sentence that hurt more than any broken toe.

Fear can be a very effective search engine. I found a new doctor, fresh out of residency, setting up shop and willing to listen. She saw me first thing Monday morning, ran labs on-site, and called at the end of the day with results: hyperparathyroidism. Translation: my parathyroid glands had gone into a biochemical yard sale, selling off my bones for cash (calcium), leaving me with pain, fragility, and brain fog.

Due to the now-constant fainting spells, surgery happened immediately. The surgeon was excellent; the nurses were cheerfully optimistic. They put me on a pain pump, but I asked them to disconnect it; I had successfully avoided pain meds for years and wasn't about to start now.

I woke at dawn the next day. The sky outside the hospital window moved from violet to lavender to a brilliant, triumphant pink. My neck was immobile from the incision (and a bit on fire, thanks to my decision to avoid analgesics), so to see the sunrise I had to turn my whole body like a stiff, awkward piece of furniture. That's when I felt something new in my limbs...nothing. I felt nothing. The bone pain had vanished as if someone had flipped a switch. I gently wiggled fingers and toes, bent joints, and savored the blessed absence of pain.

A euphoric, ridiculous joy washed over me—that pink-gold sunrise whispered, "You got a second chance–don't blow it." In that moment of sudden clarity, I realized life is meant to be lived, not squandered. Knowing that my return to the office would mean fluorescent lights, bad data, and staffing complaints, I promised myself: if a brass ring appeared, I was going to grab it like it was the last donut and run like hell.

And–the brass ring appeared.

But back to the surgery. Over the next six months, my naps evaporated. The pain never returned. My senses of both humor and direction crawled—then ran—back into service. My brain was the last to come around, but one day I noticed I no longer had to write everything down—I was remembering.

Then 2020 happened. The COVID-19 virus arrived, and I was laid off with thousands of others from my IT manager position. Job hunting during a global slowdown is a humbling sport; nobody's hiring, and cover letters start to feel like prayers. Florida re-opened earlier than most states, and I found myself wandering to estate sales to fill the hours. I loved peeking into people's homes and spying unusual finds.

At one sale, I walked up to Penny, the organizer, and impulsively blurted, "I want to work for you." She laughed—sensible, sharp, and slightly suspicious—and took me on.

I learned the craft: pricing, staging, cajoling buyers who treat small antiques like Fort Knox. I formed a deep friendship with Penny's other helper, a wonderful lady named Donna.

After a few sales, I noticed Penny looked frail. Confiding in her about the brilliant, young doctor who diagnosed me, I sat with her as she made an appointment.

Unfortunately, Penny's journey was different than mine: cancer, widespread. After speaking with an oncologist, she went directly into hospice.

Penny still had one estate sale scheduled, and she planned to give it up. Donna and I were in shock, but we put our heads together and agreed we could conduct the sale ourselves and give the proceeds to her son. Penny consented, and we ran with it.

She didn't make it through the sale. Six weeks after her diagnosis, Penny quietly passed away. I didn't have time to grieve; I learned the news sitting behind Penny's checkout desk with a line of customers standing in front of me.

The sale was heartbreaking but went well, all things considered. People began asking Donna and me to do other sales.

So I did something I never imagined: I formed a company—Posh Peacock Estate Sales—named for Winter Park, with a mission to make kindness and customer service our guiding principles.

Within months, I realized estate sales were paying my bills. Flashing back to that purple sunrise, I realized I hadn't found the brass ring; it had somehow, improbably, found me. I fulfilled my promise—I grabbed it and ran.

We grew fast. I hired an operations manager, pricing experts, and more staff, and watched the company evolve into something beautiful.

Sometimes I wonder if I'd have had the courage to start my own business without that twelve-year illness. Probably not. I was a cog in a corporate machine.

Am I a salesperson now? Small-business owner? A former IT manager with an uncanny ability to identify mid-century modern in dim lighting? All of the above. Some people are born knowing how to seize the bull by the horns; others need a shove. After twenty-five years in IT, I needed the shove. Plus a surgery and a sunrise. But better late than never.

About Melissa

After twenty-five years in the IT world, Melissa Sullivan traded fluorescent lights and bad coffee for vintage lamps and bustling estate sales. Founder and owner of Posh Peacock Estate Sales in Orlando, she turned an unexpected medical crisis into a second act: diagnosed with hyperparathyroidism after years of unexplained pain, surgery restored her health and renewed her appetite for life.

Laid off during the 2020 pandemic, Melissa wandered into estate sales, apprenticed with a local organizer, and—after running a final sale for a friend who later passed—launched the Posh Peacock, prioritizing kindness, excellent customer service, and thoughtful curation.

As a former IT manager, Melissa brings organizational rigor, a sharp eye for detail, analytical skills, and a knack for pricing to every sale. She lives in Winter Park with her family and two shih tzus, loves a good story about a found object, and believes the proverbial brass ring is worth grabbing.

Facebook: PoshPeacockEstateSales
Instagram: @poshpeacockestatesale
TikTok: @orlando.estate.sale

A Journey Built on Love, Service, and Transformation

Shiela Wyatt

In 2001, I was living in the Dominican Republic with my husband and daughter. We had relocated there to open an Outback Steakhouse—an adventure that felt exciting, but also unfamiliar. One afternoon, while visiting on vacation, my mom handed me a copy of *O, The Oprah Magazine*. Inside was an article about a professional organizer in New York City.

That moment changed everything.

As I read about the work this woman was doing—bringing order, peace, and simplicity into people's homes—I felt an immediate spark of recognition. It wasn't just interesting. It was as if the article had put into words something I had always felt in my bones: that helping people create calm in the middle of chaos was what I was meant to do.

I returned home from the Dominican Republic with a one-way ticket to Winter Park, Fla. I didn't have a business plan or an investor. What I had was conviction—and a stack of homemade flyers and business cards I printed at Kinko's. I passed them out, put them on car windshields, and trusted that someone out there would take a chance on me.

Within two weeks, I landed my first client. That project led to another referral, and then another. From the very beginning, Shiela & Co. was built on relationships and word of mouth, and I am proud to say that referrals remain the foundation of our work to this day.

Over the next two decades I would divorce, remarry, and raise four children only to divorce again. In 2021, I found myself at a point in my life I had yet to experience. Living alone for the first time in twenty-seven years—my kids had grown and started lives of their own—I had no idea who I was outside of the roles I had as a wife, mother, and business owner. I had to take this time to find out who and what my interests were NOW.

I downsized and moved into a bungalow in the heart of Winter Park, into my absolute dream house. Very soon after I moved in, I found myself overwhelmed and crying in the kitchen. I was terrified I had made a mistake by moving from our home and that my children would not feel like they were coming "home" when they visited. I realized first-hand how life transitions make one question everything. I felt alone and scared as I looked for answers about who I was and what was important to me in those moments of solitude. Creating a home that supported me and my interests was a foreign concept.

The last four years have been full of ups and downs. I have learned to live a life full of friendship, laughter, music, beach days, and travel. Business boomed and led us to travel with clients moving around the country and internationally. Both old and new friends have helped me heal and find my part of this journey: a new beginning to what has become one of my happiest moments in life. I have watched my daughter get married and become a mother herself. I have become a grandmother, and wow, is this an absolute indescribable feeling. I am witness to my other adult children becoming my best and closest friends as they share their lives and adventures with me. Every time they walk through my door, I feel them coming "home." This is what we strive to create for our clients, loving their homes.

When I first started, my focus was purely on home organizing. I worked mainly with busy women and families—people who were balancing careers, raising children, and managing households in a world that rarely slowed down for them.

As a mother myself—later a single mom raising both a daughter and a son—I understood the never-ending demands of daily life. I knew firsthand how a cluttered home could feel overwhelming, and how even a little organization could create breathing room for joy, family, and possibility.

Over time, many of my clients began asking if I could help with more than closets, kitchens, and playrooms. They needed help with packing, moving, and resettling—one of the most stressful life events anyone can face. At first, I helped out informally. Then I realized: this was not only a natural extension of my work, but also something I had been preparing for my entire life.

When I was growing up, my parents moved us forty-two times across Delaware, Texas, South Carolina, and Florida. Constant relocation gave me an eye for efficiency and a knack for creating order in the midst of upheaval. Friends often called me to help them pack and move, and while others dreaded it, I secretly loved it. Eventually, I stopped being embarrassed to admit that I enjoyed packing boxes—and instead leaned into that strength.

Today, moving management has become a cornerstone of Shiela & Co. My team and I have developed a system where, with just three or four dedicated women, we can pack an entire home in a day or two, oversee the move itself, and have our clients unpacked and settled in their new homes within a week. What once seemed overwhelming becomes seamless. What once was stressful becomes manageable.

At Shiela & Co., our work is not just about boxes and labels. It's about people.

My love language has always been *acts of service*. I believe that the most meaningful work happens when you serve others with love, joy, and genuine care. Every client we work with is more than a customer—they're a relationship. I take the time to understand their needs, their fears, and their hopes for the next chapter of their lives.

That philosophy extends to my team. I've surrounded myself with amazing women who share the same values. Together, we bring energy, empathy, and excellence into every project. We believe many hands make light work, and we pride ourselves on taking a burden off our clients' shoulders so they can breathe easier.

We don't just provide a service. We provide peace of mind.

One of my favorite parts of this work is witnessing transformation—not just in the physical space, but in how people *feel* once the process is complete.

I've seen overwhelmed moms breathe easier after their kitchens are streamlined. I've watched families cry tears of relief when they realize their cross-country move will actually be smooth. I've even had clients tell me they've slept better at night because their home no longer feels like a source of stress.

Every project reminds me why I started: because creating order out of chaos changes lives. It also reminds me of why I continue: because life doesn't stop during challenging transitions.

What began in 2001 as a one-woman operation with homemade flyers has grown into a thriving company that has helped countless families through some of life's biggest transitions.

In 2025, I found a partner and created Elite Moves—our very own moving company, based on simple values to help facilitate seamless transitions for our clients. We have an amazing team of men who not only lift the heavy loads but also care about our clients and what they are going through.

As Shiela & Co. continues to expand along with Elite Moves, my vision is clear:

- To be a trusted partner for families and individuals during times of change.
- To set the standard for moving and organizing services built on compassion, efficiency, and excellence.
- To grow a team of women who find joy and pride in serving others.
- To remind people that love can be found even in the most practical of services—packing, moving, and organizing.

At Shiela & Co., we don't just organize homes or manage moves. We create environments where people can thrive. We believe in leading with love, working with joy, and serving with purpose.

At the end of the day, we're not just moving boxes. We're moving lives. Lives that we ourselves are living. Lives that we want to share so we can connect with others and build community. I am grateful for all the transitions in my life that have brought me to where I am today: loving my life, loving my cherished family and friends, and loving our clients that we get to know so well. I look forward to more of what this journey will bring for me and my team. I am grateful to be able to share my journey. I am committed to serve with compassion, joy and purpose. Transitions are indeed stressful, but they also remind us they bring growth, new opportunities, and meaningful connections.

About Shiela

Shiela Wyatt is a highly accomplished professional organizer and philanthropist with a wealth of experience in both fields. She began her career as a professional organizer in 2001 in Winter Park, Fla. Over the years, she has established herself as an expert in creating efficient lifestyles for clients through intentional organization and space planning. She also has a special talent in managing the logistics of a move, making it a seamless experience for her clients. She owns both Shiela & Co and Elite Moves Moving Company based in Winter Park, servicing clients statewide, nationwide, and internationally.

In addition to her professional work, Shiela is deeply committed to making a positive impact on the lives of those around her through philanthropy. For nearly a decade, she has been involved with One Heart, a nonprofit organization that strives to improve the lives of individuals and families living in poverty. She leads their annual toy drives, increasing awareness and donations year after year. She also served as vice president on the Love Your Life Foundation board, which empowers individuals and families through education and community-building initiatives. Shiela is a board member with the Park Avenue District. The Park Avenue District's goal as a nonprofit is to encourage economic vitality through design and promotion within the context of historic preservation. Shiela chairs the promotions and events committee in hopes that people fall in love with the charm, sophistication, and history of the Park Avenue District.

Shiela is a new grandmother and mother to four adult children. She loves to cook and spend time on the water. She is known for providing solutions and serenity to people in both her professional and philanthropic efforts.

Beauty From Ashes

Bree Holbrook

I'll never forget sitting on that burnt orange couch with the tiny white flowers, legs swinging off the edge, staring out the window, and waiting for a dad who wasn't coming home. I was five. That was the day I learned my parents wouldn't be living under the same roof anymore.

Something shifted in me that day. I didn't have the words for it then, but a quiet lie took root: If love leaves, maybe it's because I'm not enough to stay for.

That lie became my silent soundtrack for years.

I watched my mom carry the weight of the world on her shoulders. She was exhausted, working endlessly to provide, and I remember promising myself—one day, I'll find a way to take care of my family without missing out on them.

That promise became the fire that's still burning inside me.

So I became the achiever. The straight-A student, the athlete, the girl who believed that maybe if she performed well enough, she could finally feel whole. But no matter how much I achieved, the emptiness followed.

Then, at nineteen, a friend introduced me to a different kind of love—the kind you don't have to earn. She told me about a Father in heaven who loved me on purpose, for a purpose. I cried like I'd been waiting my whole life to hear that truth. And as I began my relationship with Jesus, it changed everything.

For the next decade, I poured myself into helping others find that same hope. I mentored young women wrestling with the same questions that haunted me: Am I enough? Am I loved?

At twenty-five, I got married. We were broke and sharing our dreams on a couch we literally found on the side of the road. Then reality hit—two imperfect people with unhealed wounds. We almost broke, too. But we chose healing over quitting. Counseling. Prayer. Perseverance. That choice saved us and became one of our greatest teachers.

Then came seven long years of infertility. Month after month, I felt my heart sinking and body betraying me. The old lie whispered again: something must be wrong with me. But through those tears and prayers, God met me there. Waiting became my refining fire. It softened me, deepened me, and grew my compassion for every woman still waiting on her miracle.

And then—miracles. Today I have three children who are my everything. They're the living, breathing proof that God still writes comeback stories. Every time I look at them, I see redemption staring back at me.

In my thirties, I found myself saying yes to something I swore I'd never touch: direct sales. I was craving purpose and opportunities to influence, and even though I had doubts, I felt a nudge. I started small—and ended up finding not only success, but sisterhood. I loved watching women rise, watching belief return to eyes that had lost hope.

Ten years later, it all came crashing down. A single Zoom call. A corporate restructure. Everything I had built was gone.

But now I see it wasn't loss—it was redirection.

At forty-five, I was doing all the "right" things for my health—eating clean, working out—but my body still wasn't responding. I was exhausted, and it felt like midlife was winning. That's when a friend told me about a company pioneering a new approach to health: ingestible peptides from nature. I studied the science and knew in my gut that this was the vehicle to change lives.

Before I ever tried them, I believed in the mission. When I finally did, the shift was undeniable. My energy came back. My body felt aligned again. For the first time in years, I didn't feel like I was fighting myself.

That spark became a wildfire. I started sharing, and within months, I had a team of hundreds. Then thousands of customers. Within a year, we built a million-dollar organization built not on hype—but on hope.

I'll never forget a woman named Robin, sixty-eight years old, who told me she had tried everything and was skeptical that this would work. A few months later, she called me ecstatic. "Bree, I am down forty pounds, and the best part is that I am able to get down on the ground with my fourteen grandkids!"

That moment went straight to my heart. Because that's what this is really about.

It's not about numbers, or titles, or status. It's about giving people their lives back—helping them get their lives and dreams back.

And that's when I knew:

I don't just want to build a business.

I want to build a legacy that gives.

By 2030, I want to give away one million dollars—because we live in a world that is literally dying for hope. And I refuse to stand as a spectator.

Every dollar, every story, every healed heart—it's all part of that mission.

I believe that when women rise, families heal. Communities heal. The world heals.

So if you're reading this, and you feel like life has burned you down—hear me: ashes are where beauty begins.

You were never meant to settle for survival.

You were made to slay.

Slay your fear.

Slay your doubt.

Slay the lie that says you're too far gone, too late, or too small to make an impact.

Because God's not done writing your story.

And maybe—just maybe—the chapter you're living now is where your miracle begins.

About Bree

Bree Holbrook is a wife, mom of three, and entrepreneur on a mission to help women believe in their health, their purpose, and the power of what is possible when they refuse to settle. As a founding leader with Make Wellness, the first company to bring

AI-derived bioactive ingestible peptides from nature to market, Bree has built an organization generating over a million dollars in sales, all rooted in faith, freedom, and family. Through her movement and her message *Made for More—that you no longer have to settle for surviving*, she helps women rewrite their stories, create financial margin, and rediscover who God created them to be in body, mind, and soul.

@breeholbrook
https://makewellness.com/ED9B6F70B8

About the Curator, Leigh M. Clark

Four-time best-selling author Leigh M. Clark is known for her inspiring books, including *The Dream is in Your Hands*, *Living Kindly*, and the *Slay the USA* series. Her work as an author has empowered and motivated countless readers by highlighting kindness, resilience, and the strength of community. In addition to her writing career, Leigh has over 20 years of experience as a business strategist, working with Fortune 500 companies to help them grow and succeed.

Leigh's latest project, the Slay the USA series, is a growing national movement that shines a spotlight on extraordinary women across the country who are leaving their mark on their communities and industries. Through this series, Leigh is empowering these women to share their stories of triumph, leadership, and impact, much like she has done in her own life. The series is rapidly expanding, highlighting women in cities from coast to coast, celebrating their contributions and inspiring others to follow their lead.

Leigh's expertise and passion for leadership and empowerment have made her a sought-after speaker, with multiple appearances on the TEDx stage. Her stories of kindness and personal growth have been featured in prominent publications like *HuffPost* and shared through appearances on *The Today Show* and the *Rachael Ray Show*.

As the founder of Kindleigh, a movement focused on giving back through acts of kindness, Leigh has led initiatives that have raised significant funds for charitable causes. Her mission is to create lasting change through kindness and sharing stories of impact, further solidifying her role as a leader in philanthropy.

Leigh resides in Southwest Florida with her son, Carter, and the love of her life. She's here to make an impact and leave her mark by illuminating others.

"Don't let the world change your heart. Let your heart change the world." - Leigh M. Clark

Instagram: @leighmclark @slaytheusa
www.leighmclark.com
www.slaytheusa.com

www.ingramcontent.com/pod-product-compliance
Lightning Source LLC
Chambersburg PA
CBHW061743120626
46550CB00005B/1873